THE LISTENING VOICE:
AN ESSAY ON THE RHETORIC OF SAINT-AMANT

FRENCH FORUM MONOGRAPHS

40

Editors R.C. LA CHARITÉ and V.A. LA CHARITÉ

For complete listing, see page 139

THE LISTENING VOICE

AN ESSAY ON
THE RHETORIC OF SAINT-AMANT

JOHN D. LYONS

FRENCH FORUM, PUBLISHERS
LEXINGTON, KENTUCKY

319284

c C

Library of Congress Catalog Card Number 82-82429

ISBN 0-917058-39-9

Printed in the United States of America

For Patricia

TABLE OF CONTENTS

PREFACE

One of the ironies of literary history is that its failures are often the result of a profound complicity with the authors and movements that seem to be its victims. Saint-Amant, as *égaré*, as *grotesque*, or as *écrivain indépendant*, would be delighted at the way in which his own playing with the forms and themes of history is echoed in history's ways of playing with him. We are all familiar with the traditional descriptions, current since Boileau, of the poet of the taverns, scrawling his verses with a coal on the wall. This biographical legend would seem to be too charmingly naïve for comment, if, on the one hand, it did not appear with disquieting frequency in the studies of modern scholars and if, on the other, it did not derive from a specific and habitual rhetorical strategy of Saint-Amant that deserves further study.

The persistent reading of Saint-Amant's texts as unserious, random constructions or as simple transcriptions of sensory experience can be divided into two categories. The first views the poems as a *simulacrum* of the author's state of mind and state of soul. Odette de Mourgues writes of the "myopic" and "disconnected" vision of the *libertin* poets—Saint-Amant, Théophile, Tristan l'Hermite—and sees their work as being largely confined to descriptive or occasional verse in which a rhetorical disunity is the symptom of a deeper moral disintegration. The reader can hope at most to find little gem-like felicities of expression: "Their way of coming almost irrelevantly upon a delicate flower or a moon beam gives a magic touch to the isolated object."[1] *Le Contemplateur* and *La Solitude*, Saint-Amant's most widely known texts, are "playful daydreams connected only by the whims of the poet's fancy."[2] Imbrie Buffum, kinder to the *libertins*, absolves them of amorality in order to lodge them in his Christian baroque. But he too finds in their works, even the *Contemplateur*, which he calls Saint-Amant's masterpiece, no logical plan. The only unity of such poems, Buffum argues, is "organic" and based on the temperament of the poet: like Montaigne, Saint-Amant jumps "from one picturesque subject to another." For Buffum, the taste for vivid "multiple-sense" experience determines most of the poems' imagery.[3] Decrying the failure of earlier scholars, Francis Lawrence reopens the search for "unifying factors" but paradoxically finds that *La Solitude* and *Le Contemplateur* are a succession of "intensely felt, detached moments."[4] Lawrence's description of the poems depends entirely on the debatable assumption that the poem is in some way the direct communication of sensation, a descriptive assumption closely tied to a causal and biographical assumption: "For Saint-Amant, then, there is no God continually thrusting his creative power between man and nothingness. In the place of God, the only things that hold Saint-Amant from non-being are feelings, sensations, and whatever causes sensation. He exists by means of sensation. He flings himself from one sensation to another."[5] These readers of Saint-Amant conclude that the works can only be dealt with as a whole by seeing an equivalence between Saint-Amant's mental process at the time of composing and the organization of the text. In the version of the "fallacy of imitative form"[6] that underlies these readings, the whimsy and craving for intense sensation assumed to characterize the poet's mind are conveyed, it seems, directly in his words. Typical of this view is the observation that in *La Solitude* the "consciousness of the poet leaps from one phenomenon to the next without placing either the object or the reaction in a logical hierarchy."[7] This direct equivalence of poems and experience appears in a comment on *Le Contemplateur* as well: "The appearance of a fresh object in the sea wrenches Saint-Amant's attention back from the sky."[8] The critics' search ends in an assumption about the poet's mind, and the specifically literary phenomena that constitute the text seem to vanish.

The second tradition of reading, also exemplified by approaches to *La Solitude* and *Le Contemplateur*, has looked through the poems to the external circumstances of the poet at the moment of the poem's composition and not to the poet's mind. Françoise Gourier[9] sees in *La Solitude* an account of the poet's activities and occupations in a country retreat at Belle-Ile. She describes it as an "Ode à la Nature," marked by its great precision in the depiction of a specific locality and its vegetation. Jean Lagny, Saint-Amant's eminent biographer and editor, also regards his poems as direct evidence of the author's experience in specific places in the historical world.[10] For this school, the primary debate over poems like *La Solitude* has concerned the establishment of the precise geographical location described in the text. This reading has been seriously challenged by the work of the German scholar Wentzlaff-Eggebert, whose work on *La Solitude* documented the many textual borrowings from pastoral novels and poetry of the early seventeenth century in which similar "landscapes" are described. Thus, the "experience" of the poet, previously assumed to be external and historical, appears to be a reworking of traditional literary motifs.[11]

A variant on the assumption that Saint-Amant is recording the external world by creating verbal references to non-verbal experience is the "pictorial" reading. In one sense, this method of reading the poet has been the most rewarding, for it has underlined the author's real interest in the painting of his period, his allusions to specific paintings and to favorite subjects of the period that appear in painting, in prints, and in literature, and his thematic use of the problems of the interaction of the verbal and the visual in such texts as *L'Andromède*. However, the limitations of pictorialism in describing Saint-Amant's work are most evident in the words of one of the proponents of this reading. Of *La Solitude* C.D. Rolfe writes that "the somewhat bewildering array of little scenes does prevent one from deciding just how to take the poem."[12]

Readers, then, have generally found Saint-Amant's work disordered and fragmented, have deplored this characteristic of his poetry, but have nonetheless promoted the poet to a prominent position in works of literary history and anthologies. They agree rather oddly that he is a good but naïve and careless writer. Can such readings in any way guide us towards an appreciation of Saint-Amant? Yes, insofar as it is instructive to consider what has troubled earlier readers. They seem to make the equation of author with speaker and then to have difficulty with the relationships (1) between the person addressed (designated reader) and the poet on the grounds that the qualities ascribed to the receiver of the poem seem exaggerated or inappropriate (e.g., in *Le Contemplateur*); (2) between the poet and his experience in the scene described (e.g., in *La Solitude*); (3) between the objects in the scene and the general "meaning," whether this be considered as logic or thematics. Two steps seem necessary to resolve the problems of earlier readings. First, the assumption that the historical author and the speaker are one and indissoluble must be suspended. Secondly, some attention must be given to the rhetorical nature of the text, for, if the speaker is not the biographical poet, the organization of what is presented to the audience may have some coherence other than an experiential one. The patterns, conceptual and verbal, of the poems can perhaps be seen as borrowing from the historical world, but the texts need not be reduced to or collapsed into this external realm.[13]

My hypothesis will be that the difficulties of readers derive from the rhetorical stance taken by Saint-Amant in almost all of his work. As author he creates an internal speaker who seems to be producing the poem but who is in fact a character in the poem's fictions. Of course, the first-person speaker is the most frequent grammatical voice of the lyric, but in the speakers of Saint-Amant there is a consistent and very prominent distancing and fragmentation of the poem's theme, achieved through an emphasis on the speaker and his characteristics. Frequently, the poems are about the act of composition itself. But even when they are not explicitly centered on the act of writing, the organization of the poems around a certain kind of speaker calls into question the values and patterns of poetic language: its mirroring of the person addressed, its representation of symbolic objects, its explicit assumption of the social exchange that produces poetry, and its criticism of the social concepts of reality and event. The result is a poetry that is always ironic and critical but never blunt or revolutionary in dealing with social and religious concerns. Saint-Amant's texts are oblique, always containing a larger dose of self-critical perspective than of social virulence. They frequently deal with religious and military-historical themes in a subversive—that is, a lucid—way, but they always call the poem and its own voice into deeper perplexities and doubts than they do any of the external conventions of the social world.

This rhetorical pattern, which I will attempt to describe, is responsible for the kind of reading that Saint-Amant has been given. Readers have fallen into the "scene of the poet" and not gone beyond. They have sensed the importance of the *persona* but not looked at the patterns into which his presence falls, patterns which, as the poet's marionette, this character acts and speaks.

Before proceeding, it may be helpful to specify the meaning of "rhetoric" in this study. Aristotle defined the function of rhetoric as being "to discover the available means of persuasion in a given case."[14] These means include three categories of proof: proof based on the characterization of the speaker, proof based on the awakening of an emotional response in the hearer, and proof based on a demonstration or apparent demonstration in which the speech itself seems to take precedence over the speaker or hearer. Now the application of rhetoric, which is, for Aristotle, a branch of political science, to poetic texts is obviously a selective process. Persuasion or demonstration of the truths or probabilities useful in deliberative, judicial, or even epideictic proceedings are clearly not equivalent to the use of discourse in poetic activity. Yet, poetry shares with other discourse the basic relationship between maker and receiver of the text. It is furthermore significant, for our purposes, that the first two of the three kinds of proof should be based on the emphasis on the character of the speaker or on the emotional state induced in the listener. My reading of Saint-Amant's poetry will be devoted to discovering the ways in which the poet makes use of the fundamental author/reader relationship, and more specifically the ways in which his poems constitute representations of that relationship.

The rhetoric of all poets is not the same, nor is the rhetoric of a single poet the same in all his poems. However, there are sufficient constants in the ways Saint-Amant relates author, reader, and text—the three components of the rhetorical process —for us to emphasize the characterization of rhetoric as the discovery of the available *means* of persuasion, rather than as the practice of persuasion itself. It is true that there are here two senses of the term "rhetoric," one the study of the means—a study which Paolo Valesio suggests we call *rhetorics*—and the other the exercise of these means before and upon an audience. Saint-Amant's usual stance is to unveil the *means* at his disposal, the means by which he can inform, praise, imitate, or otherwise exercise a certain power over an audience. His is a rhetoric which is therefore constantly ironic and constantly revelatory of the artifice of poetic invention and of the rules of the social hierarchy within which the inventive activity is deployed. In other words, if one wished to adopt Valesio's terminological distinction, one would call Saint-Amant's a rhetoric of rhetorics. I will instead prefer the metaphor of the *listening* voice—an attempt to designate the poet's attentiveness to the forms and means of discursive relationships, an attentiveness which appears in the critical interplay between production and reception in the organization of the poems themselves.

In saying that the poet represents the relationship of author and reader in the text, I am claiming neither that the *persona*, the speaker who says "I," is necessarily entirely different in every way from the historical author of the poems nor that the "I" is identical to the historical author. The characteristics of the author and of the "I" or speaker are made available to us as readers primarily by the evidence internal to the text. To understand the relationship between poet and public in a text means, therefore, to take into account many things besides the qualities and actions attributed to the speaker, the figure Wayne Booth[15] calls the "dramatized author." The "implied author"—to follow further Booth's terminology—is a reflection of many other choices besides those directly related to the speaker and among those choices are things apparently outside the control of the speaker —events that befall him, apparent contradictions in his words, etc. Much of the difficulty in dealing with Saint-Amant's rhetoric comes from the willingness of many readers to allow the "dramatized author" or speaker to dominate their descriptions to the point that it is difficult to discern any difference between this speaker and the implied author (or even between the speaker and the living person who was the writer—that is, the biological person who existed outside and beyond these texts). The present study will attempt to profit from the ample and vivid characterization of the speaker that is typical of Saint-Amant's work but will also seek evidence of the qualities of the implied author.

The representation of the author-reader relationship must, however, take still other elements into account, for the audience of a text, as inscribed in the text itself, is fully as complex as its creator. It includes the explicit addressee or designated audience, who is named in the text and is frequently a benefactor of the poet. This designated audience may be single or multiple and may be given greater or lesser degrees of realness or historicity. Next to this designated audience, however, there is an implied reader who is not excluded by the first audience. In fact, quite frequently the praise addressed to a designated audience is intended for public presentation and only attains its full value when the passive and unnamed implied reader is assumed to have access to the text. Neither of these two audiences is fully identifiable with historical persons, for they are both creations of the text. In the text, these audiences may be used to *refer* to historical entities, but such reference does not make historical persons fully equivalent to their textual counterparts. While Cospéan, the designated audience of *Le Contemplateur*, is also a historical contemporary of Saint-Amant, the qualities of Cospéan as they are known to us from sources other than the poem are not necessarily coextensive with those attributed to him within the poem. At the very least the characteristics of the designated audience within the poem will be only a selection from among those historically knowable. Similarly, the historical public of the poem, a certain part of the educated seventeenth-century population, may very well have influenced the writer's design of the implied reader, but the implied reader will not fully coincide with such an historical population. Again, there will be a selective vision at the very least; there may also be a deliberate distance imposed between implied and historical readers.[16]

The present study of Saint-Amant's rhetoric will concentrate on the organization of texts as it reveals an interplay between the designated audience and the speaker, on the one hand, and the implied reader and the implied author, on the other. By studying primarily texts in which the "scene of the poet" or explicit representation of a speaker gives us a point of departure, I hope to be able to use this speaker as a key to many other components of Saint-Amant's rhetoric. For this speaker, once we no longer grant him the privilege of identification with the author, is a very important clue to the way the whole text works.

The relationship between the historical writer and the historical public (and hence between the implied author and the implied reader) is determined by a number of conventions. One of these is the social and economic hierarchy which creates patterns of exchange, patterns which will take on great importance in our readings of individual texts in this study. Another convention, one which calls for some preliminary remarks here at the outset, is that pact between reader and writer known as literary genre.

One of the peculiarities of Saint-Amant's work, an aspect of his poetry that removes the interpretive support that we often have in reading poetry of the Renaissance and Late Renaissance, is that its generic affiliations are unclear. The importance given to genre in the writing, reading, and evaluation of poetry in the sixteenth and seventeenth centuries is clearly shown by its place in the treatises of *ars poetica* of Castelvetro, Minturno, Vida, Scaliger, Du Bellay, Sebillet, Pelletier, Colletet and Boileau.[17] But in the work of Saint-Amant we seek in vain texts illustrative of the established and noble genres. We find instead *caprices*, such vaguely defined (or undefined) genres of lyric production as elegies and letters, epigrams (even an *épigramme endiablé*), and the two great "heroic idylls." The only way in which genre can be a clue to the reading of Saint-Amant is in the indication of the poet's refusal of the restrictions imposed by genre. His verses evade the usual classifications and, if much of his work can be called *burlesque* or *grotesque*, it is apparently because of a desire for the freedom permitted in the lowly and unregulated. As Saint-Amant said, he wanted elbow room in language.[18]

The variety of the works he published between 1629 and 1661 demonstrates how generic heterodoxy was a permanent

constituent of Saint-Amant's work. Heterodoxy, but not igno-
rance. From *La Solitude*, which he designates himself as his *coup
d'essay*, to the *Moÿse sauvé* (1653) and *La Généreuse* (1658), his
two "heroic idylls," the poet deftly uses the chromatics of generic
classes. *La Solitude* is not a pastoral poem in the Theocritan-Vir-
gilian mode (dialogic) nor a *soledad* in the Gongoran sense.[19]
Rather, Saint-Amant's poem founds a new genre, one that has
passed into literary history with its celebrated mate by Théophile.
Towards the end of Saint-Amant's career, the heroic idylls, perhaps the very best of his work, mark a similar and more explicit
refusal of strict adherence to genre. They are not epic; yet they
treat of matters that transcend most epics in importance, aspects
of the salvation of mankind. They are not bucolic; yet they treat
of those "noble subjects under humble guises" that merit the
appellation *idyll*. Both outside the poems—in his letters to the
reader and his notices—and within the poems themselves, Saint-
Amant considers the constraints imposed by generic decorum
upon language and conception and claims for himself the freedom
of the humble, the intermediate, and the uncertain.

In reading Saint-Amant and in inviting others to read him with
me, I want to explore the ways in which the poet represents
poetry itself as a process, mediation, exchange. Seeking to stim-
ulate in the reader implied by this rhetoric a consciousness of
these activities, Saint-Amant distances himself from his matter.
He reserves for himself the right to an ironic irresponsibility for
what he says. He traces the lines of literary tradition and of the
social conditions that determine his forms of address. He underlines (and undermines) the social function of the art of poetry
in an age of monumentality and hierarchy. And most of all, he
places squarely before us the problem of the relationship between
language and event which remains a problem for much modern
criticism.[20] These characteristics of Saint-Amant's work can be
seen in what I would group in three major forms of the speaker's
rhetorical stance: as figure in a natural landscape or seascape; as
participant in a feast; as reporter of heroic military event. These
divisions in no way constitute stable classes or "modes."[21] They
are simply clusters of examples in what the tradition has isolated
as Saint-Amant's best work, and they reveal three specific metaphors around which the poet builds his speech.

Chapter I

CONTEMPLATION AND SECULAR PRAISE

Le Contemplateur, like much of Saint-Amant's poetry, is based on elaborate and ironic use of a traditional form of discourse, religious meditation. The influence of meditational practices on the thematics and structure of the lyric in sixteenth- and seventeenth-century Europe has become clear since the publication of the studies of Louis Martz and Terence Cave and has inspired numerous studies of the devotional lyrics of French poets.[1] Daily meditation or meditation undertaken during set periods according to the detailed instructions of manuals such as those of Ignatius of Loyola, Luis de Granada, and Luis de la Puente provided believers with an individual means of making their daily lives the theater of divine revelation.

Saint-Amant seized upon this conventional, highly codified, and very popular genre in two of the poems which have assured him a place in literary history. One is *La Solitude* and the other *Le Contemplateur*. Their similarities of structure are great: an apparently random movement of a first-person character in a seacoast landscape within which designated objects assume a certain metaphoric sense. Saint-Amant must have felt that he had not realized to the full the possibilities of this structure in what he termed his *coup d'essay*.[2] In returning to it in *Le Contempla-*

teur he indicated more explicitly, both in the title and in the text itself, a reference to the meditative practice which it exploits.

Le Contemplateur is extremely complex both because of the nature of its generic reference and by virtue of the rhetorical maneuver involved in transforming a devotional work into a witty secular offering for the designated audience, Saint-Amant's benefactor, the bishop Philippe Cospéan. It is useful, therefore, to review briefly the basic elements of contemplation or meditation. This devotional practice is generally subdivided in the early seventeenth century into three activities. The first of these is the composition, the imagining of some place, event, or attribute connected with the life of Christ.[3] The second activity of the meditator is the analysis, through which he attempts to grasp the significance of the object that he has so vividly imagined in his composition.[4] Finally, in a "colloquy," the meditator addresses God, a saint, an attribute of God, or some other entity of religious significance in supplication, prayer, promise, or exhortation. These three activities, which were subdivided into steps that could make actual meditative practice quite complex, correspond to a tripartite division of the powers of the soul into imagination (or memory), understanding, and will.[5] In the usual sequence the culmination in the colloquy is the occasion for the mediator to engage himself emotionally and take a position in regard to his own actions or to make an outpouring of gratitude or contrition. While these activities appear ordinarily as steps in a sequence, they can be combined.[6] Furthermore, when meditational practice is used as the basis of lyric composition, the different activities, strictly separated or not, may receive varying emphasis. For instance, as Terence Cave notes, in the early seventeenth century the demand for a *dévotion aisée* led to "a reduction or even an omission of the analytic element, and hence of figurative or emblematic images."[7]

A further distinction is often made between the evening and the morning meditation, the first a penitential contemplation of sin, often based on the Old Testament, and the second a meditation on the New Testament, particularly on the events of the Passion and Resurrection.[8] In Ignatian meditation a distinction is not made in terms of evening or morning but in the distribution of subjects through the different weeks, beginning with a meditation on the first sin, the sin of the angels, and ending, in the seventh week, with the Ascension of Christ into heaven forty days after his resurrection.

At the beginning of *Le Contemplateur*, in an address to Cospéan, the poet establishes the thematic key to the poem by praising the bishop as an instrument of salvation and then announces that the form of the poem will be that of a trial. The designated audience of the poem is told that during this performance the poet's ability in the invention and disposition on concepts will be displayed in "ces Vers, / Où d'un art pompeux et divers / Je feray briller mes pensées; / Et croy que les plus grands Censeurs / Les verront si bien agencées, / Qu'ils en gousteront les douceurs" (vv. 25-30). To judge from many readings, these clues to the organization of the poem—the juxtaposition of the address to Cospéan as "sainct Orateur" (v. 5) and with the announcement of a performance that must be judged for its technical skill—have not yet been followed very far.[9] As a result, the extremely successful integration of the representation of poetry as a mimetic activity (the imitation of the designated audience by the speaker) and as a social exchange has more often than not been seen as a rather disordered accumulation.

The text, organized syntactically around the speaker, is usually summarized by enumerating the actions that he attributes to himself. The speaker of *Le Contemplateur* evokes in this narrative or "scene of the poet": (1) his perceptions from a high rock overlooking the ocean, where he looks at birds, the sea, fish, a dove, a boat, a nest, and an *homme marin*, a creature resembling man, fish, and god; (2) his activities on shore and on the surface of the sea after his descent from the promontory (hunting, fishing, reading, collecting shellfish, finding his way in the dark); (3) his evening activities in the manor with his host, his reading and writing of poetry, including sacred poetry, before going to bed; (4) his awakening the next morning and his looking at the sun rise. This summary deprives the poem of its complex, many-leveled nature, for the narrative of the first person only provides the most superficial framework of the text. On the level of this narrative, however, we can see a fairly simple spatial and temporal patterning: (a) outside/inside/outside (in reference to the manor house), (b) higher/lower (in reference to the promontory), (c) chronological (early to late over a period divided into day/night/day). On the narrative level of the first person, the poem does give a sense of coherence reinforced by the apparently cyclical character of (a) and (c) ([b] will be considered later) and even at this level does not deserve quite its portion of blame for randomness.

The poet's creation of this order is, however, challenged from within the text by the many reminders of its factitious and composite nature: "Tantost lassé d'estre en repos / . . . / Tantost je tire aux Cormorans / . . . / Tantost nous allant promener / . . . / Quelquefois, bien loing écarté / . . . / Quelquefois surpris de la nuit" (vv. 191, 195, 201, 211, 215). The dispersion of these many different times is barely held in check by the overall anecdotal order in which they are grouped according both to spatial association (e.g., activities of the lowlands and sea level—fishing, hunting, etc.) and to the temporal fiction of a diurnal progression. There is thus a tension, on the level of the "I," between a first linear or horizontal unfolding and a second vertical superimposition of different events that are designated as collected from different times and condensed for presentation into a composite day.

There is, though, a level on which the chronological unfolding of the text is strong and consistent, a contemplative level that appears if we leave the first-person narrative to observe the content framed by (but absent from) the speaker's passage through time and space. What I call the "contemplative" level here could be further defined as a fusion of the composition and analysis of meditative technique. The two, frequently expressed as separate phases in devotion, can be so intertwined that they are, in practice, simultaneous. When this fusion occurs, the figurative significance of each contemplative object is conveyed along with the imagination or description of the object. To attempt to categorize the various sections according to an emphasis on one or the other activity would, I think, deflect attention from the underlying unity of the contemplative level (I will refer to the third of the contemplative activities, the "colloquy," separately).[10]

We are guided to the discovery of this contemplative level by the very limited number of objects designated in the segment of the poem concerned with the speaker's presence on the promontory: birds, ocean, fish, dove, ships, sky, Halcyon's nest, *homme marin* (strophes 5-19). These objects, moreover, except for *l'homme marin*, are not described—there is no enumeration of their qualities—but simply designated as "being there." They serve as links or *points de repère*, tying into the narrative of the speaker the contemplative discourse. This other discourse is marked repeatedly as being imaginary or as dealing with the intangible and the absent. The poet's opening remark on the promontory ("Là, par fois consultant les Eaux / Du sommet d'une roche nuë . . .") leads to an imaginary conversation with Thetis about the limitation imposed on her waters by God:

> Mais elle m'en dit la raison,
> C'est que le respect qu'elle porte
> A Dieu qui l'a mise en prison,
> Ne luy permet pas qu'elle en sorte:
> Il suffit qu'elle ait autrefois
> Logé ses Monstres dans les bois
> Pour aider à punir nos crimes,
> Et qu'elle ait surpassé les monts,
> Pour nous plonger dans les abismes
> Où trébucherent les Demons.
> (vv. 51-60)

The following strophe evokes the experience of Noah during the Flood, designated as the speaker's representation of this scene to himself, before this contemplative sequence is reattached to the seascape by the mention of a dove: "Puis voyant passer devant moy / Une Colombe à tire-d'aile, / Aussi tost je me ramentoy / L'autre qui luy fut si fidelle . . ." (vv. 71-74).

These opening strophes of the section in which the speaker is represented as being on the promontory manifest the primacy of the contemplative level over the anecdotal level, for the appearance of the dove is generated by the thematics of the Flood.[11] Noah, if his biblical narrative were condensed iconographically, would certainly be left with an ark, a dove, an olive branch, and these are the objects included in the contemplative level. The dove which appears in the anecdote of the speaker follows the appearance in the poem of Noah. Hence, the anecdote is more clearly directed by the contemplative than vice versa, since the speaker's thought is echoed by, or inscribed in, the seascape. The adventures of the "I" become an apparent motivating framework for the biblical reference. The contemplative moves forward thus with occasional attachment to the first-person anecdote. Within the former level of the poem we find the third temporal series mentioned above, for the Flood of strophes 6, 7, and 8 is followed at the close of the poem by the Apocalypse of strophes 34 through 45. This chronological progression of a macrocosmic dimension is reinforced by a similar progression in human events from Aristotle (strophes 9-10) to current political events (strophes 27-28). There is even a reference to the anteriority of Saint-Amant's own *La Solitude*, thus setting the text as a whole into a chronological sequence of an order quite different from that of the cataclysm of biblical history: "Tout ce qu'autrefois j'ay chanté / De la Mer en ma Solitude, / En ce lieu m'est représenté . . ." (vv. 151-53).

We are thus confronted with a macrocosmic chronology, a factitious microcosmic one, formed out of many superimposed instants which maintain a certain centrifugal tension, and another time, potentially the most obvious but frequently confused with that of the anecdote of the speaker—the time of the saying of the text itself, the meta-discursive time in which the poet intervenes, comments upon, and reverses the direction of his words. Each of these temporal orderings corresponds to a distinct level of the text in terms of the speaker's relationship to the content of his speech: meta-discursive (speaker commenting on his act of speaking), anecdotal (speaker as character of a narration), and contemplative (the thematic or "philosophic" content). What I have called the contemplative level is by far the largest (in simple terms of number of strophes allotted to it). Even though it is second by its fictive distance from the scene of the speaker (a temporal and modal discontinuity), there is no reason to consider it as inferior to the narrative which frames it and weaves through it. Furthermore, it is necessary to make some account of the contemplative if we are to understand the meta-discursive, for the latter, at the end of the poem, comments upon the former.

A summary of the seascape section of the poem in terms of contemplation yields a rather different view of the poem from that available in an outline of the speaker's actions: the ocean encloses fish and is enclosed within the limits of the shore by God's will (strophe 5); in the past it covered the mountains and filled the woods with fish to help God punish man's crimes (strophe 6); mankind took refuge in the first boat (*logis flottant*) made by Noah, whose tears stopped the Flood (strophe 7); a dove, the incarnation of the Holy Spirit announced peace to Noah by selecting an olive branch from among many trees (strophe 8); the speaker assumes the language of the Philosopher and penetrates the secrets of nature (strophe 9); the speaker becomes lost in the mysteries of the flux and reflux despite a desire to understand as ardent as that of the Philosopher, who drowned himself in the Euripe (strophe 10); the speaker fails to understand the principle of the magnetic compass that guides ships and of the attraction between the magnet and the north and iron (strophe 11); this attraction of metal to metal is stronger than that of friendship among men of the present day (strophe 12); the Duke's friendship for the poet disproves the foregoing (strophe 13); the Halcyon's nest floats undisturbed under the happy influence of three personified forces of nature (Aquilon, Saturn, Phoebus)(strophe 15); the poet describes the sea-man (strophes 16-19).

The section on the Apocalypse and Last Judgment (strophes 32 through 43) need not be described in detail here, since it does not run the risk of being read as part of an anecdotal experience as do the aspects of contemplation that are intertwined with the scene of the speaker in the first part of the poem. It is, however, frequently chopped into small details (by Buffum, in particular) without regard to its role in the poem as a whole. If we look at the contemplative as a level that runs throughout the poem, the coherence of *Le Contemplateur* is much more evident, and it is even more tempting to see the anecdote as pretext for the thematic content of the contemplation. When it is juxtaposed with the opening strophes of the poem, the closing Apocalypse reveals the basic antithesis on which the poem is based: water versus fire. The earlier section of the poem (strophes 5-19) is an exploration of the mysteries of water, while the final strophes (strophes 32-44) exalt the power of fire. The religious mysteries of the Flood and of the Last Judment are thus interpreted in the form of that favorite of Late Renaissance figures, antithesis, in which Gérard Genette has seen the key to the "baroque" imagination.[12] By using it thus, Saint-Amant projects the temporal progression from past to future into what has long seemed a permanent opposition transcending time, the mysterious affinity and combat of fire and water. The contrast of these two elements is a spatial one (cf. "L'Autre allentit le feu d'Amour / Qui dans l'Eau mesme le consume," *La Solitude*, vv. 57-58) and can appear only when the mind is struck by the incomprehensible synchrony of hostile elements. For its effect, antithesis requires more than simple juxtaposition; there must be a structure of cohesion that permits the incompatibility to manifest itself. In *Le Contemplateur*, the two elements are not in equilibrium, for they are incorporated into a thematics of destruction—thus there is a common function in which they can be compared—and the "high element" of fire at last triumphs over the sea by burning it. The antithesis is pushed to its furthest extension by the complete reversal of the relationship of the two elements, a reversal that is only taken half-way in most antitheses (i.e., water destroys fire [norm] → water and fire coexist → fire destroys water).

The poet carefully underlines this process and organizes around it the two major contemplative sequences, for the destruction of water by fire is a "revenge" of all that was menaced by water:

> Les Metaux ensemble fondus
> Font des rivieres precieuses;
> Leurs flots boüillants sont espandus
> Par les campagnes spacieuses.
> Dans ce feu, le dernier des maux,
> Tous les terrestres Animaux
> Se consolent en quelque sorte,
> Du Deluge à demy vangez
> En voyant ceux que l'onde porte
> Aussy bien comme eux affligez.
> (vv. 421-30)

The fire versus water motif appears thus in many variants and produces a new version of the opening Flood. The fire takes the form of a liquid—the "flots boüillants" of the molten metals—and covers the earth as did the sea in strophe 6; the sea animals that lived in the woods during the Flood are in their turn destroyed by the new wave of fiery liquid. With this anaphoric reference to the opening strophes, it seems difficult to overlook the general organization of the poem and not to see that with the Apocalypse the active but stable nature of antithesis has yielded to a dialectic in which both of the opposing elements are destroyed. Fire destroys water and then destroys itself, just as death destroys all and then itself.

This reversal, which closes the compositional-analytic phase of the text (prior to the colloquy), is part of a pattern established within the exploration of the water mysteries. Reversal of antithesis is the basic process by which the poem moves forward. In the opening strophes on the promontory there is a series of reversals involving both the speaker and the scene:

> Là, par fois consultant les Eaux
> Du sommet d'une roche nuë,
> Où pour voir voler les oyseaux
> Il faut que je baisse la veuë:
> Je m'entretiens avec Thetis
> Des poissons et grands et petis
> Que de ses vagues elle enserre,
> Et ne puis assez admirer,
> Voyant les bornes de la terre,
> Comme elle les peut endurer.
>
> Mais elle m'en dit la raison,
> C'est que le respect qu'elle porte
> A Dieu qui l'a mise en prison,
> Ne luy permet pas qu'elle en sorte:
> Il suffit qu'elle ait autrefois
> Logé ses Monstres dans les bois
> Pour aider à punir nos crimes,
> Et qu'elle ait surpassé les monts,
> Pour nous plonger dans les abismes
> Ou trébucherent les Demons.
>   (vv. 41-60)

The speaker's position is marked by its anomalous height, for he is far above the birds. It is this anomaly *in itself* that is important here, not the possible visual consequences. There is no allusion to the potential perspective over vast expanse of water (as there is in *La Solitude* and in much Romantic landscape). Thetis as ocean encloses fish and is in her turn enclosed by the coast. Thus the reversals terrestrian/aerian and encloser/enclosed open the contemplation of the water mysteries in strophe 5, and the Flood of the following strophe is the result of a redistribution of these roles. During the Flood, the place of the aerian creatures in the woods was taken by the aquatic creatures now enclosed in the ocean; ocean itself covered (enclosed) the mountains that now enclose ocean. The position of the speaker in the present, on a mount overlooking birds and water, is reversed to provide the image of humanity during the Flood plunged into the abyss. The contrast in time between the mythic past and the poetic present is translated into a rearrangement in spatial relationships between the various objects and the speaker.

After the development of the founding destruction, so to speak, which plays over the relationships of this anomalous spatial situation—the floating "house," the tears that stop the Flood, instead of adding to it—the poet passes to another spatial reversal in his relationship to the water by assuming the encloser/enclosed dichotomy that earlier characterized the ocean itself. He "descends" into the terms of the Philosopher, his curiosity "fathoms" all of the secrets of nature, "Et dans ma recherche profonde je loge en moy tout l'Univers" (vv. 89-90), he says. This metaphoric enclosure of all, reusing the term for the ocean's filling the woods with fish (*loger*), is followed immediately by the reversal of that figure precisely while the poet is contemplating the example of reversal itself in the ocean:

> Là, songeant au flus et reflus,
> Je m'abisme dans cette idée;
> Son mouvement me rend perclus,
> Et mon Ame en est obsedée:
> Celuy que l'Euripe engloutit,
> Jamais en son cœur ne sentit
> Un plus ardent desir d'aprendre:
> Mais quand je veux bien l'esplucher,
> J'entends qu'on n'y peut rien entendre,
> Et qu'on se pert à le chercher.
> (vv. 91-100)

The closing strophes of the section of the poem in which the speaker is on the promontory are devoted to the only descriptive sentences of the "seascape." But—and this is a reminder of the way in which the spatial situation of the speaker is generated by the contemplative level and not by a pictorial recording—even more than the other objects assigned to the external world of the poem, the sea-man is without an evident visual or perspectivist relationship to the speaker-viewer or to the other objects of the seascape. The sea-man section is set off, furthermore, by a particular insistence on the artistic or artificial nature of his representation. Saint-Amant makes an allusion to his *Solitude* and presents the earlier text as the original of what is here represented or re-represented. This allusion to verbal/textual presentation is followed by the mediation of the visual arts, themselves present only metaphorically, not only for the product of the printed image, but as the process by which the image comes about:

> Tout ce qu'autrefois j'ay chanté
> De la Mer en ma Solitude,
> En ce lieu m'est représenté,
> Où souvent je fay mon estude:
> J'y voy ce grand Homme marin,
> Qui d'un veritable burin
> Vivoit icy dans la memoire:
> Mon cœur en est tout interdit,
> Et je me sens forcé d'en croire
> Bien plus qu'on ne m'en avoit dit.
> (vv. 151-60)

The mention of the *burin* is ambiguous. It can be read as saying "engraved *as* with a veritable chisel" (i.e., "etched in memory") or as "engraved with an accurate chisel" (i.e., "truthfully presented in an engraving"). Whether or not we privilege one of these readings—one purely metaphoric and the other metonymic and meta-discursive—the phrase accentuates the process of engraving over the product of that gesture. Finally, the speaker becomes the relay between past words about the sea-man and the reader, to whom he conveys an amplified vision, "Bien plus qu'on ne m'en avoit dit." The sea-man is thus set off from the other objects of the sea section by a heavy foregrounding of the media: earlier poetic text, engraving, and the language in which the poet has heard about this creature and which is insufficient, thus forcing the poet to go beyond what has been said.

The description that follows continues to emphasize the artificial and precious aspect of this creature. He exists at the juncture of nature and non-nature, the point at which the accumulation and arrangement of substances found in nature surpasses the natural order: "il empoigne un Cor / Fait de nacre aussi rare qu'or" (vv. 175-76); his plumage is made of "mainte branche de coral / Qui croist sous l'eau comme de l'herbe" (vv. 181-82); he has as a scarf "Vingt tours de perles d'Oriant" (v. 185). While he is at the frontier between nature and non-nature, the sea-man is also at the point where humanity and non-humanity overlap: "Il a le corps fait comme nous, / Sa teste à la nostre est pareille" (vv. 161-62); "Bref à nous si fort il ressemble / Que j'ay pensé parler à luy" (vv. 179-80). And these contrasts are held together by the reference to the process of artistic creation that opens the passage, a phenomenon recalled as *process* rather than as finished object: "Un portrait qui n'est qu'ébauché / Represente bien son visage" (vv. 171-72).

This complex, long, and rather startling description has been catalogued by biographical criticism as a reference to a sea lion![13] But the text thoroughly undermines any such referential intent and indeed questions the basis of the zoological interest in such creatures by emphasizing the process of assembly of a similitude of man in natural substance. The sea-man is above all a work of *art* on the frontier that Saint-Amant explores at length in the poem and which is the narrow and precarious border between sense and nonsense that appears in tropes—antithesis, oxymoron—and in object. *L'homme marin*, whose name itself is oxymoronic, is an image of man remade in precious substance. He is not natural, he is not human, he is man projected into the element which in the first half of the poem is the most hostile to mankind.

The portrait of the sea-man is based on a "making-strange" or "defamiliarization"—Shklovsky's concept is fully appropriate here.[14] In rhetorical terms, defamiliarization is a procedure by which the adherence of the audience to the representation is not encouraged by a careful adjustment of statement of prevailing opinion but instead made difficult in order to force the audience to reexamine two things. One of these is the world of everyday experience transformed by the act of representation. The other is the process of the aesthetic work itself. Such a procedure is here doubly ironic because the image which is "defamiliarized" is not simply that of any object at all, but that of the species to which the audience belongs. The portrait begins with similarity only to move progressively into the non-human:

> Il a le corps fait comme nous,
> Sa teste à la nostre est pareille,
> Je l'ay veu jusques aux genous,
> Sa voix a frappé mon oreille;
> Son bras d'escailles est couvert,
> Son teint est blanc, son œil est vert,
> Sa chevelure est azurée;
> Il m'a regardé fixement,
> Et sa contenance assurée
> M'a donné de l'estonnement.
>
> (vv. 161-70)

The first four verses do not detail unlikeness, but instead insist on similarity. Paradoxically, this emphasis on likeness creates a suspense and perhaps a strangeness more haunting than the explicit attributes that follow; by saying that his body and head are like ours, Saint-Amant makes that ordinariness seem suspect, since it is made against an assumption that the creature is not like us. But then the body, human in its general structure, is shown to be different in substance and accident (blue hair, scaly arms). In his enumeration of the creature's panoply, Saint-Amant finds aquatic equivalents for terrestrial objects. The horn is made of mother-of-pearl, "aussi rare qu'or" (that is, it is assigned contextually a value equivalent to the most precious of the substances of dry land); he has, like the terrestrial hunter with his horn, dogs, but they are "chiens de mer," and the coral of his plumage is the aquatic variant of grass.

In its length this section on the sea-man stands out from the promontory section of the text which it ends, and no reader of the poem has ever attempted to explain how it fits into the overall thematic organization. And yet the process of projection and reversal is here fairly evident. The interplay along the contours of things which earlier appeared in the relationship between sea and land in the Flood, then in that curiosity of the Halcyon's nest which is a paradox of nature—a bird's nest that floats, the lasting counterpart to the sea creatures living in the woods during the opening cataclysm—is here continued, expanded, and concluded with the projection into the sea of the image of man himself, whose structure endures the transubstantiation.[15]

Saint-Amant, in playing here on the projection of man's image into the sea, invokes a variant of a *topos* much used in the early seventeenth century, the mirror. The sea-man passage is closely related to the Echo/Narcissus themes of the period. They are contained here as traces in this passage, especially in the reciprocal stare of the speaker and the creature—"Il m'a regardé fixement, / Et sa contenance assurée / M'a donné de l'estonnement." The allusion to *La Solitude* just before this description invites a comparison of the two poems at this point. The earlier poem contains, just after the descent of the speaker from the promontory, an evocation of similar sea treasures—ambergris, diamonds and "mille autres choses de pris"—as well as sea creatures, Tritons and Neptune. These substances are disaggregated by the action of water and storms into fragments: "Des gens noyez, des Monstres mors, / Des vaisseaux brisez du naufrage" (vv. 157-58). Immediately after this presentation of a fragmentation agreeable to the speaker, *La Solitude* presents the other, contrary aspect of the sea as a calm reflecting surface where the sun looks at itself and "on est quelque temps à sçavoir / Si c'est luy-mesme, ou son image" (vv. 167-68). Two motifs of the sea-man passage in *Le Contemplateur* are presented separately in *La Solitude*: the mirror and the sea treasures. There is an advance in *Le Contemplateur* towards completion of structures that had been begun or sketched in *La Solitude* (a tendency evident in *Le Contemplateur*'s completion of the Flood/Fire panorama). The substances are assembled into a likeness of the viewer in *Le Contemplateur*, and thus the working-out of the problem of the relationship between speaker and seascape has become explicitly a forming of the scene on the model of the speaker's own image.

The sea-man section points backwards towards the Flood, but also forward towards the Last Judgment. Like the former it contains a reversal of sea and land creatures; like the latter it involves a mutation of the human body. But in the temporal scheme of the text, the sea-man, like the king-fisher's nest, is achronic. The

Deluge is a founding and unrepeatable anomaly, while the Last Judgment is the unrepeatable moment of a mutation of the body from its past state, the prelude to Eternity. The floating nest and the sea-man are recurrent or enduring paradoxes which refer anaphorically and cataphorically to the temporal anomalies that open and close the contemplative level of the text. Because they belong also to the intemporal mysteries of the world, the two aquatic versions of things of the land are not discordant with two other phenomena with which they are juxtaposed, the flux and reflux and the magnet. Each one of these objects contains an apparent incompatibility: flux and reflux (contradictory movement), magnet (mineral hardness with animate sympathy), Halcyon's nest (aerial and aquatic), and sea-man (terrestrial and aquatic).

If we continue to read the text in terms of contemplation, we can see that these mysteries of things that seem out of place or that escape from the usual categories are linked by the speaker's tracing of the contours of the human.[16] Both the flux and the reflux and the magnet are incomprehensible to him. In trying to understand the first, he passes from confidently containing the universe within himself (strophe 9) to being drowned in the sea like Aristotle (strophe 10). When he attempts to master the concept of magnetism, which gives guidance to ships, he gets all mixed up ("mes esprits en ce discort / S'embroüillent dans la sympathie / Du fer, de l'Aymant, et du Nort"). These two mysteries lead thus to the failure of human reason, both the speaker's and Aristotle's, but the second one provides an opposition to the failure of human emotion as well:

> Là, considerant à loisir
> Les Amis du temps où nous sommes,
> Une fureur me vient saisir
> Qui s'irrite contre les hommes:
> O mœurs! dis-je, ô monde brutal!
> Faut-il que le plus fier metal
> Plus que toy se montre sensible?
> Faut-il que, sans te réformer,
> Une pierre dure au possible
> Te fasse honte en l'art d'aymer?
> (vv. 111-20)

After the intervention of the figure of the Benefactor, the two following mysteries are happy ones. The Halcyon days are a recurrent conjunction of happy influences—the influence of the Benefactor has thus altered the negativity of the magnet passage, creating a moment of human peace in the midst of the cosmic panorama of the text—and the sea-man is a positive projection of man's body into the sea (as compared to the negative projection of *engloutir* in strophe 95).

Let us now follow the signs that point towards the end of the poem. In the long section on the Last Judgment (strophes 35-44), Saint-Amant begins to tie together the Flood theme of the opening strophes, the transformation of the body, and the mediation of the visual arts as it appears in the sea-man passage. The passage on the Apocalypse begins in an apparently very casual way when the speaker claims to observe the rising sun:

> Tantost levé devant le jour,
> Contre ma coustume ordinaire,
> Pour voir recommencer le tour
> Au celeste et grand Luminaire;
> Je l'observe au sortire des flos,
> Sous qui la nuit, estant enclos,
> Il sembloit estre en sepulture;
> Et voyant son premier rayon,
> Beny l'Autheur de la Nature,
> Dont il est comme le crayon.
> (vv. 301-10)

It would seem at first that the contemplative level is being determined by the anecdotal scene of the speaker—that he was inspired to think of God by seeing the sun rise. But this strophe is between the strophe in which the reading of the Scriptures led to a sympathetic understanding of the Bible and the strophes in which the Last Judgment appears as it did in the paintings of the great "Roman," probably the Florentine Michelangelo.[17]

If we set the strophe of the "rising sun" against the preceding strophe of nocturnal reading, we can see the network which generates the pictorial Last Judgment:

> Tantost d'un son qui me ravit,
> Et qui chasse toute manie,
> La sainte Harpe de Davit

Preste à mon Lut son harmonie,
Puis jusqu'à tant que le sommeil,
Avec un plaisir sans pareil,
Me vienne siller la prunelle,
Je ly ces sacrez Testamens,
Ou Dieu, d'une encre solemnelle,
Fait luire ses hauts Mandemens.
(vv. 291-300)

David's harp lends its music to the Lute of the profane modern poet; the sacred overcomes the erotic poetry of the previous strophe. The voice of the speaker, however, is represented as giving itself over to another voice, as borrowing the idiom of another text. The spontaneity of the speaker's words is shown to be a product of the interaction with previous texts. But more striking is the chain of metaphors of authorship that follows. God is represented as the author of the Testaments, of which the ink (dark) makes his commandments shine. The light/dark antithesis links this authorship with the title "Autheur de la Nature" in the following strophe, since this authorship is also made apparent in the contrast between the dark of night (and death) and the bright ray of morning that is the sketch or portrait (*crayon*) of God. By the allusion to God's metaphoric writing of the Testaments in ink (v. 299), Saint-Amant gives concrete substance to the vision of God as writer in such a way that the title "author" (in strophe 31) takes on the resonance of "writer," even though, denotatively, the "authorship of nature" has nothing to do with writing, but only with founding or originating. The cleverness and complexity of this chain of figures appears in the opposition between the revelation of the dark ink and that of the bright sun (*crayon*).

In terms of the universal analogism and the scriptural meditation on which Saint-Amant is drawing, the two authorships are perfectly orthodox. The world does contain the message of God and the scriptures are written by God—the prophets are only his scribes. But what the poet has managed to do here, by his heavy emphasis on the artistic and artificial character of both scripture and the world, is remove the sense of immediacy in the contact with God and the world. In fact, the text of *Le Contemplateur* becomes itself a web of allusions to various mediations—David's harp, the poet's Lute (the poet thus arranges for himself an authorial image both within and outside the scriptures, a duplication of the duality in the authorships of God), the ink of the scriptures, the portrait or sketch of God in the sun. The result is a loss of the personalization and internalization that is sought in much meditative poetry and a loss as well of the permanence and authority that might inhere in the symbols through which God reveals himself. Most important, however, is the flight of any original or natural object of reference from the poem. The passage on the Last Judgment that begins here, introduced by the *crayon* metaphor of the rising sun, proceeds through a "reading" of the images of an absent painting. The poet thus distances the vision from the experiential and concrete, for he is only imagining an image already imagined by a painter. We, as readers, have before us not a picture, but the interpretation of a picture which is generated by the idea of a judgment and by a dominant rhetorical tendency to antithesis, a trope that provides the semantic equivalent to rhymes in the continuing chain of the poem.

Although many readers have insisted on the "picturesque" quality of this section, there is little attempt to create an accumulation of visual detail.[18] Instead, what Saint-Amant gives us at length is the interpretation of a minimum of spatial (gestural) elements: "Cestuy-là joint les mains en haut / Implorant la faveur divine; / Et l'autre est à peine levé, / Que d'un cœur devot il s'encline / Devers l'Agneau qui l'a sauvé" (vv. 356-60). Here the body is only designated for its actualization of codes of gesture. The process of giving interpretive models increases as the poem goes on, and there are finally antithetical pairs of the kind that remind us of Saint-Amant's earlier exploration of categories of elements in the sea passage. Strophe 37 is an example of the interpretation of a similar "posture" (recumbent couple, male and female, side by side) through two hypotheses of kinship:

> Prés de là, le frere et la seur
> Touchez de ce bruit dont tout tremble,
> D'estre accusez d'inceste ont peur,
> Pour se trouver couchez ensemble:
> Icy la femme et le mary,
> Objet l'un de l'autre chery,
> Voyans la clarté souhaittée,

Semblent s'estonner et gemir
D'avoir passé cette nuictée
Sans avoir rien fait que dormir.
(vv. 361-70)

There is little "visual" detail here, except the spatial juxtaposition of the sexes, but only an interpretation of the possibilities offered by such juxtaposition.[19] As the poem continues, the juxtaposition of opposites becomes more pronounced until we see true reversals: the lame run, the rich are poor, the mute speak, etc.

Conceptually, the resurrection is a reversal that is a manifestation of divine judgment. It is part of the future counterpart to the Deluge, which was the consequence of a judgment ("à punir nos crimes," v. 57). The qualities attributed to the risen dead are thoroughly symbolic, for they are outward representation of the internal qualities that will be judged:

Bref, en cette apparition
Ceux qui bien-heureux doivent estre,
Sans aucune imperfection
Je me figure voir renestre:
Mais les meschans desesperez
Pour qui desja sont preparez
De l'Enfer les tourmens énormes,
Ne se representent à moy
Que si hideux et si difformes,
Que mon Ame en transit d'effroy.
(vv. 391-400)

In this way, the poem continues to play with levels of the symbolization of the religious truths that are the thematic basis of the poem, for the corporal manifestation of the goodness or badness of the risen is, within the contemplative level, analogous to the appearance of Noah's Dove in the scene of the speaker. But the resurrection is only part of the symmetry of the Deluge/Apocalypse level of the poem, for the arrival of the fire completes the opposition fire/water and goes beyond antithesis to arrive at a final cancellation of the objects that served as the matter of the speaker's contemplation.

The spatial scheme of the poem is also symmetrical, for the Flood in the version we find in Le Contemplateur was a rising of the lower element, water, from its place in the ocean, into the trees and over the mountains, while the Fire comes as the falling of the stars (strophe 42) and the triumph of "le haut Element" (strophe 41). The end of the poem is also, as we have seen, the revenge of the land animals over the sea animals.

So far we have been following the contemplative level of the poem but, if this is a convenient way of dividing the text for description, it is clearly not possible to separate this level from the other levels in the reader's experience. The macrocosmic chronology that obeys its biblical and philosophical thematic and its symbolic space interacts through the text with the more limited microcosmic chronology and space of the "scene of the poet." This interaction is both conceptual (working within the largest semantic components of the text, e.g., choice of the Halcyon's nest) and lexical (the twin puns of the magnet passage, where *Aymant* and *sympathie* are given two meanings, one selected from natural philosophy, the other from human emotions). In our experience of the text the two levels are thus practically inseparable because of the overdetermination of all of the vocabulary and concepts. The magnet was chosen by virtue of its belonging to several pertinent categories: scientific enigmas, maritime equipment, sources of guidance, and attraction (*sympathie*) and for its homophonic qualities. It therefore fits the framing narrative of the speaker's presence on the promontory, offers witty antithesis between the guidance normally provided and the poet's losing his way, follows easily from the problem of flux and reflux, and provides a metaphoric base for the supposed "hardness" and "insensibility" of mankind. The flux and reflux similarly fit the framing narrative and the contemplative thematic, but also—on the third or meta-discursive level—offer a model for the speaker's explanation of the way in which he relates to the object of contemplation (at first containing and then contained in the mysteries of nature, vv. 89-92) and for the way he assembles his discourse, itself moving in two opposed directions:

> Voilà comme en me reprenant
> Avec ces dernieres parolles,
> Sur mon bon-heur m'entretenant,
> Je rends les premieres frivolles:

Voilà comme selon l'objét
Mon esprit changeant de projét,
Saute de pensée en pensée:
La diversité plaist aux yeux,
Et la veuë en fin est lassée
De ne regarder que les Cieux.
(vv. 131-40)

This allusion to the way in which the speaker's words are in some way free and reversible is comparable to the declaration of randomness that is made in connection with the conversation at the table of the Duke (strophes 26-28). But, however much the poet claims unpredictability for the character of his fiction, the poem as a whole shows a particular determination of the thematic by the address to the audience. The relationship between speaker and audience was said earlier to be one of the problems encountered in reading this poem. But this problem does not arise because of any inattention to the audience on the part of the poet. On the contrary, it arises because we modern readers are no longer comfortable with such extensive reference to the audience, that is, to the powerful patrons to whom Saint-Amant's poems are dedicated and addressed. Having experienced more recent literary movements that advocate independence of art from social utility or that view art as a means of improving the world through disinterested teaching of truth, we are uncomfortable with texts that are explicitly part of a hierarchical relationship. We are acutely embarrassed to find that the text does not claim to be disinterested. We are more used to a rhetoric of accusation; hence the enduring effect of the Baudelairian *hypocrite lecteur*. For the poet of the Late Renaissance—and this is particularly the case with Saint-Amant—it was quite common to reflect within the text one of the conditions which gave it value, its belonging to an exchange. The representation of the benefactor within the text is not so much like the use of a vocative to open a conversation as it is an inscription of the sort that one finds in monument and painting bearing the name or image of the donor. The work contains therefore two different images, one serving as object or matter of the work, the other the sign of the intervention or stimulus that caused that object to be realized in an artistic work. Both images are subjected to the same overall procedures of representation—verbal, graphic, plastic.

Despite the various indications of the distinctions between the two kinds of image within the work—difference in costume, lighting, color (in painting), difference in grammatical person (second-person vocative and imperative versus third-person, etc.) in the text—there are frequently interferences between the two to permit either a thematic or a dramatic interaction. The donor, in a religious "Adoration," for example, may have the posture of an authentic participant in the biblical scene and thus function dramatically within the work. Or the donor's life may contain an episode manifesting one of the virtues that is characteristic of a particular saint, and this thematic resemblance may be displayed by a juxtaposition of the two scenes.

But the representation of the donor or benefactor reveals a relationship to the maker of the work as well as to the object (which need not, of course, be a religious object; it can be civil, military, erotic, etc.), and the length and repetition of allusions to this relationship gives it a considerable influence on the impression made on the reader of the text. As if the repeated allusion to one benefactor were not enough, Saint-Amant in many texts—for example, *Le Cidre* and *La Généreuse*—inserts a second benefactor within the poem and thus creates a kind of mirroring or *mise en abîme* of the poet-benefactor relationship. In *Le Contemplateur*, the action of exchange between Cospéan and the poet which is performed in the opening (1-3) and closing (46) strophes of the poem finds a replica in the relationship between the speaker and his host, the Duke in Belle-Ile (strophes 4, 13, 26-28). The speaker is thus between two benefactors. He demonstrates within the text his way of relating to a benefactor and also *performs* that same relationship within the poem as a whole (an example of an illocutionary-perlocutionary couple, where the poet exemplifies—inner image—and performs—outer image—what he has exemplified).

Near the center of the text appears a demonstration of the power of verbal invention over an audience. Claiming to entertain the Duke, the speaker recapitulates some of the motifs of the immediately preceding action:

> Treuvay-je au retour couvert-mis,
> J'entretiens mon DUC à la table,
> En-tant comme il me l'est permis,

De quelques propos delectable:
Je le fay rire de ma peur,
Je luy dy quel spectre trompeur
J'ay creu s'estre offert à ma veuë;
Et pour noyer tout mon soucy,
Sur un grand verre je me ruë,
Où le vin semble en rire aussi.

Là, suivant les sujets du temps,
Tantost nous parlons de la Digue
Où, vray Prophete, je m'attens
De voir crever la jeune Ligue:
Tantost, les cœurs tous réjoüis,
Nous celebrons du Grand LOUYS
L'heur, la prudence, et le courage,
Et disons que le Cardinal
Est à la France dans l'orage
Ce qu'au navire est le fanal.

(vv. 251-70)

These strophes and the following one about the English fleet provide a key to the rhetorical process which gives form to *Le Contemplateur*. The words of the speaker and the "experience" that these words attribute to the speaker as character are selected in view of the pleasure of the receiver. The specter, which was "believed" to exist in proportion to its nonexistence (v. 240, "Je croy voir tout, pour ne voir rien," cf. v. 159, "je me sens forcé d'en croire / Bien plus qu'on ne m'en avoit dit"), is the matter of the "propos délectable" which will provoke the internal receiver's laughter, a laughter which is made possible by the fictional nature of the event recounted. The distance between the possible reality and the represented and emphasized non-reality ("spectre trompeur," "pour ne rien voir") is the speaker's gift to the host whose pleasure is his goal. This is a relationship by antithesis, in which the fictive and fictionalized fear of the speaker provokes the laughter of the listener. Such a relationship is made possible by a *dédoublement* of the speaker, who undermines the referential status of his words by the heavy insistence on the *failure* of perception that he imputes to himself. Furthermore, this "exchange" is encoded in the substance of the social ceremony that unites speaker and listener, wine: drowning care/ laughing wine. The speaker thus permits the receiver of the tale to participate in the process of the amusements by assuming the role of the critical (and superior) half of the two-part game of the speaker. This strategy of two viewpoints on a common theme is followed by the union of speaker and listener in a common discourse, the military and naval themes in which the "I" is eventually replaced by a unifying person: "Et disons que . . . / Nous projettons." The speaker thus finishes by adopting the matter of predilection of the receiver (military, political subjects) and uniting poet and receiver in the process of producing the language of the text. In *Le Contemplateur* as a whole, the language of the dinner conversation is distanced inwardly from the address to Cospéan since the present tense of the speaker's and Duke's designated conversation is not, of course, the present time of the speaker's address to Cospéan.

This representation near the center of the text of the poet's participation in a language characteristic of the audience provides a relay of the opening and closing comments on the language of the audience of *Le Contemplateur*, Cospéan. Saint-Amant seems to be demonstrating within the poem the kind of mirroring or sympathetic elaboration of the discourse of the receiver that typifies the text as a whole. Cospéan is a "sainct Orateur" (v. 5) whose "paroles choisies / Sont autant d'articles de Foy" (vv. 9-10). The survey of the eschatological verities which furnishes the poem's basic structure is a projection of a holy oratory into the framing discourse of the speaker's micro-temporal existence. The speaker's contemplation reflects Cospéan's words and the contemplation is contained in germ in the first strophe of the address to this benefactor:

> Vous, par qui j'espere estre exemt
> De choir en l'eternelle flame,
> Apostre du siecle present,
> Cause du salut de mon Ame,
> Divin Prélat, sainct Orateur,
> Juste et souverain Destructeur
> Des infernales Heresies;
> Grand Esprit, de qui tout prend loy,
> Et dont les paroles choisies
> Sont autant d'articles de Foy.
>   (vv. 1-10)

The choice of qualities attributed to Cospéan has motivated some questioning of Saint-Amant's sincerity. It is true that many of the epithets applied to Cospéan could equally well be applied to God himself ("Juste et souverain Destructeur / Des infernales Heresies"; "Grand Esprit, de qui tout prend loy," etc.) as could the closing assertion of the poet, "je suis vostre adorateur" (v. 460). The problem of sincerity in historical terms escapes the reading of this text alone and even the juxtaposition of all of Saint-Amant's poetic texts. But the rhetorical structure of *Le Contemplateur*, when compared to other texts that play a similar game (e.g., *L'Andromède, L'Epître au baron de Melay*), provides a kind of "syntax of address" that would be used whether or not the poet is sincere in some biographical sense. It seems that the relationship between speaker and audience is based on an imitation of the audience, the assumption by the speaker of the function of the person for whom he constructs the text. The "conversation" with the Duke gives an example of this, but the thematic contemplation is even more revealing, for the poet at length recapitulates certain "articles de Foy." At the end of the dedicatory section, Saint-Amant provides a schema for this use of language when he tells Cospéan, "[vous] meritez qu'en chaque lieu / On vous fasse part aux loüanges / Que vous-mesme rendez à Dieu" (vv. 18-20). Sincere or not, the praises of Cospéan fit the pattern of reflection of the bishop's praises to God.

The order of generation of the levels of the text seems to run, then, from the language of the audience to the theme and hence to the anecdote of presentation or "scene of the poet":

ADDRESS → THEME → ANECDOTE
.
.
.
[address → theme]

(where the profession and preoccupation of the audience of the poem determine a thematic which is framed by a certain anecdote, and where, in *Le Contemplateur*, a secondary movement from address to theme is inserted *within* the level of anecdote [relationship to Duke]). Insistence on these levels may seem to be laboring a point. However, the persistent tendency of critics of Saint-Amant to assume tacitly that the content and form of the poem were the inevitable result of the presence of the poet in a certain place makes such insistence necessary in order to liberate poetic discourse from historical document.

There is something more in *Le Contemplateur* than the simple pleasure of writing in a way that provides a pleasant and clever mirror for the audience. To create a work which exemplifies the relationship between different social classes is to participate in the broader social function by which these relationships are translated into objects and in which the social order manifests itself as aesthetic object, to create a monument. The Late Renaissance and Baroque periods are dominated, in painting, sculpture, and architecture, by the creation of works with the function of imposing a certain social hierarchy and view of history. Literary texts can be considered as creating in the reader social attitudes analogous to those instilled by the fine arts. One aspect of the monumental—generally dealt with in literary criticism as the "occasional" or "official"—in poetry is the demonstration by the writer of respect for the audience (sponsor or benefactor) of the text. This is part of the social purpose of the monument. As Giulio Carlo Argan has expressed it, "The fundamental quality of the monument is its representative function. It always possesses an ideological content and meaning, and because it aims at representing the stability of certain ideal values, it is always expressive of the principle of authority and its historical basis."[20] But the monument must go beyond the historical, for it is not simply a record or reminder but an Incitement to follow an example and to join the chain that is both historical, existing in different periods, and contemporary, existing in the hierarchy of the present. One way to move the viewer to follow an example is to make the monument itself a performance of obedience to the powerful.

The particular way in which the relationship of speaker (maker) to receiver (sponsor or benefactor) is inscribed in the work around a theme is a public ostentation (without any pejorative connotation). The implied reader (viewer) of such a work is not the person openly and explicitly addressed—in this case Cospéan—but an unnamed public which "overhears" an address to the benefactor. The result is an exaltation of the benefactor or explicit audience. This exaltation is achieved in many ways, in part by the simple juxtaposition of the benefactor's name with the thematic content of the work, in part by a metonymic relationship in which the theme, as here, stands for a quality of the benefactor, and in part by virtue of the existence of the monument itself, the value of which "earns" distinction for the benefactor since he is in some way the cause of this work of art now available to the public.

In its will to create an attitude of respect, already inscribed into the work by the relationship between the maker and the sponsor, the monument can propose a longer chain of expressions of respect in which the sponsor takes part. In the exaltation of Cospéan in terms that seem exaggerated, we see a displacement of the qualities of God onto those of his servant and an application to the servant of the language he applies to God: "qu'en chaque lieu / On vous fasse part aux loüanges / Que vous-mesme rendez à Dieu" (vv. 18-20). This chain reappears in the two closing strophes where the speaker addresses both God and Cospéan in a language of prayer:

O Dieu! qui me fais concevoir
Toutes ces futures merveilles,
Toy seul à qui pour mon devoir
J'offriray les fruits de mes veilles,
Accorde-moy par ta bonté
La gloire de l'Eternité,
Afin d'en couronner mon ame:
Et fay qu'en ce terrible Jour
Je ne brusle point d'autre flame
Que de celle de ton amour.

Et vous, dont les discours sont tels,
Accompagnez des bons exemples,
Que par leur fruit les vrais Autels
Triomphent de tous les faux Temples:
Vous, dis-je, à qui j'escry ces Vers,
Où dans la mort de l'Univers
Un haut renom s'immortalise,
Vueillez estre leur Protecteur,
Et permettez-moy qu'on y lise
Que je suis vostre adorateur.

(vv. 441-60)

The two strophes offer a striking parallel: the poem seems to be offered simultaneously to both God and Cospéan and to be

offered to each one exclusively ("Toy seul à qui . . . J'offriray"/
"Vous . . . à qui j'escry ces Vers"). Each begs a certain return or
compensation for an offering ("Accorde-moy . . . Et fay . . ."/
"Veuillez . . . Et permettez . . ."). What could seem simple con-
tradiction is given coherence by the distinction in grammatical
person (toi/vous). The function of each of the audiences is distinguished as well, for God is asked to provide a purely spiritual
protection against eternal damnation. Cospéan, on the other
hand, as the choice of the hierarchical and distancing vous indicates, is asked to give a worldly protection for the poet and his
verses against other men. Cospéan's words and actions are effec-
tive, not directly in the absolute realm of eternal salvation, but
in the temporal domain of combat against false doctrines that
are abroad in the world. Moreover, the earlier of the two strophes
does not contain an explicit mention of the result of the poet's
labors in language, though the future "fruits of his vigils" certainly implies his poetry. The final strophe of Le Contemplateur,
on the other hand, is quite dominated by references to language
—discours, j'escry ces vers, un haut renom, qu'on y lise—and its
effects—triumph and immortalization. The difference between
the two strophes consists in a change of level that distances the
text as a whole, as self-conscious object created for an offering,
from the contemplative core. This distancing, of course, undermines the apparent spontaneity or sincerity of the contemplative
center and makes us realize that all that precedes was conceived
(in Saint-Amant's terms) in virtue of its destination.[21]

Returning to the direct address with which the poem began,
the speaker completes the performance which he had set for himself as a goal in the second strophe. By the end of the poem it is
clear that the poet is capable of being a "sainct Orateur" as well,
or, at least, of imitating one, for the concluding strophes, one
addressed to God and one to Cospéan, complete the structure
of a contemplative poem. They constitute a form of colloquy,
that movement by which the "soul speaks intimately with God
and expresses its affections, resolutions, thanksgivings, and peti-
tion."[22] This description of the colloquy fits precisely the penultimate strophe, "O Dieu! qui me fais concevoir / Toutes ces
futures merveilles." As for the last strophe, it can be read as a

colloquy, for meditators address themselves to saints, attributes, or even abstractions, and Cospéan could be considered here an instrument of God (though at the same time this strophe can be read as an *envoi*, returning to the secular aspect of Cospéan). Saint-Amant thus completes his use of meditative form, for his work does not only contain composition, analysis, and colloquy, but follows the distinction between the Old and the New Testaments, assigned to different days and even to different times of day. The first day is devoted to sin, vanity, and punishment: to the casting of the devils into hell and to the Deluge. It concludes in the evening with the mention of David's harp and of the Testaments.[23] On the morning of the next day begins the meditation on New Testament events. In this way a division between evening and morning meditations is maintained. If one compares the scope of Saint-Amant's subjects of meditation to those in the Ignatian manual, one finds that they begin with aspects of the same event (the first sin, that of the rebellious angels, who were cast into hell) but that Ignatius ends with the ascension while Saint-Amant moves on to the resurrection of the dead and the end of the world, omitting the Passion.[24]

The concluding strophes serve, however, another function besides that of concluding the meditative form. They comment on the discourse of the poem itself. In a first layer, the Apocalyptic scene is the object of a meta-discursive commentary on the inspiration and its value as first fruit in future offerings for salvation, and then another layer of meta-discursive commentary offers all that precedes, including implicitly the penultimate strophe, to a temporal power openly concerned with the social effects of language. The text thus underscores the nuances between a religious and atemporal offering and the monumental presentation to Cospéan, whose position on earth may derive from God's power, but who is concerned nonetheless with the distinction between the mortal and immortal in language and representation.

Yet one may very well wonder whether the effect of the respectful dedication is precisely that of instilling respect. *Le Contemplateur* uses many of the structures of the monumental —its opening and closing praises and dedication, its representation of the social hierarchy and the role of the artist, its pretensions to unite the doctrinal past and future in a single work of art—and themes common in monuments of the period—the Flood and the Apocalypse of the Sistine Chapel, the military and naval exploits of King and Cardinal—but it hardly produces conviction or unhesitant adhesion.

The final strophe has a great part in producing this sense of distance and indeterminacy. The conclusion of *Le Contemplateur* has in common with *La Solitude* the revelation of the entirely social nature of its poetic language, the link between the language of the intended receiver and that of the poem. In *La Solitude* this conclusion can be seen as a surprise to the extent that it undermines the spontaneity simulated in the opening verses ("O que j'ayme la Solitude! / Que ces lieux sacrez à la Nuit, / Esloignez du monde et du bruit . . .") of absolute solitariness. In the intricate dialectic of the close of *Le Contemplateur*, the poet ironically takes back exactly what he gives, for the immortality that he offers Cospéan is written with the matter of destruction itself—"la mort de l'Univers"—so that in a sense the reading of the final strophe is a wager.[25] If one believes in the speaker's acceptance of the doctrine of the end of the world, then one may assume his sincerity but in doing so undermine the value of the purely literary immortality he offers. If one believes that the speaker has simply used a colorful cosmological framework from Christian doctrine, then the immortality promised may very well be the only immortality, but his offer of it is built on a conscious fallacy.

This indeterminacy evidently conflicts with the insistence in the opening and closing strophes on the destruction of falsehood. Cospéan's success in driving out false doctrine and in propagating the true one projects upon the text a disconcerting dichotomy. Saint-Amant's poem seems unlikely to create in the reader a conviction of the value of official doctrine. One need only compare La Ceppède and Saint-Amant to feel a profound difference. Yet the text begins and ends with emphasis on the triumph of true over false altars; it contains numerous allusions to the problems of guidance and confusion (the compass) and of true perception and report (the nocturnal illusions, the reports about the sea-man). But the text's insistence on the borrowing of the language of others ("les termes du Philosophe," v. 84, the assumption of the language of the Duke) and on the effects of art (the sea-man, the painting of the Last Judgment) creates for the poem and its speaker a privileging of the ordering and representative functions over judgmental ones. This reading seems emphatically recommended by the speaker himself when he says, "Je feray briller mes pensées; / Et croy que les plus grands Censeurs / Les verront si bien agencées, / Qu'ils en gousteront les douceurs" (vv. 27-30). The distinction between true and false is the business of Cospéan, the poem's audience, but the use of those categories, borrowed from the discourse of the audience, to create patterns in language is the business of poetry.

Chapter II

FEASTS

We have been invited, throughout the ages, to many literary feasts. The metaphorics of such celebrations are rich and varied enough to bear many different conceptions of the community and of the poetic act. Yet the intricacies of Saint-Amant's use of this concept have rarely been given scrutiny because of many readers' habit of viewing the "gastronomic and bacchic"[1] poems as biographical—Saint-Amant revealing himself as the carefree reveler or *goinfre* of so much literary history—and merely descriptive of various real botanical fruits and dairy products. These poems are subject as well to a tacit moral condemnation that, having made the biographical assumption, goes on to equate personal lack of integrity with textual disintegration. In Boileau's eyes, a poet "Ainsi tel autrefois qu'on vit avec Faret / Charbonner de ses vers les murs d'un cabaret"[2] was unworthy to approach the altar of high seriousness. But *Le Melon, Le Fromage, Le Cantal, Le Cidre, La Crevaille*, and *L'Epître au baron de Melay* are poems of great complexity and thoughtfulness. Their wit merits a more attentive public, attentive to the gestures of the speaker as well as to the qualities of the titular object of the feast.

Discourse—I follow here Benveniste's use of the term—is centered on the subject, on the one who speaks.[3] Whether the speaker's presence is made explicit by use of the pronoun "I" or whether it be revealed less directly through the use of certain adverbs, verb tenses, etc., relationships in discourse are established between persons and objects in reference to this speaker. The speaker defines himself while defining his audience and his object. An imperative, for instance, conveys a certain definition of the speaker who utters it, even in the absence of other sources of information about the speaker. This implicit self-definition, in the case of the imperative, may not fit what we know about the speaker from other evidence (a lowly speaker could demand that a king obey him), but it is the way in which relationships are defined *within* the discourse. In the lyric, the power of the speaker to define himself is increased enormously by the traditional disconnection of the lyrical subject from external (extra-textual) definitions of the speaker. The lyric is structured outward from its "I" towards the second person, or receiver, through reference to the categories of time and place that define the relationship—and thus, in a circular fashion, define the "I" itself. In much, perhaps most, lyric, the speaker does not name himself, or indeed, the other persons. Yet, and this is the case with Saint-Amant, even when the speaker *does*, with great emphasis, include his name in the text, the lyric affords the speaker a particular freedom of self-definition and thus an unusual degree of ascendancy over the other persons and objects in the speech situation.

However, what have been called the gastronomic and bacchic poems of Saint-Amant add to this ordinary discursive centering a second kind of centering on the "I." The speaker participates in a specific activity, the feast, radiating from the couple formed of the transcendent speaker and the object of the feast. Let us consider the feast, as it grows out of and involves the speaker, the role of the object—fruit, cheese, wine, and ham—and the tropes, in particular the metaphors, that are generated by the interaction of subject and object.

The main structural fact of these poems, one that has occasionally been overlooked, is that they are not primarily descriptions of a food, but accounts of the exchange and consumption of food and drink.[4] This activity, furthermore, is emphasized by its duplication. Many of the poems are divided into two levels of enunciation, on both of which there is an exchange, production, or consumption of food. There is a first level of the poems in which the speaker, in his discourse, describes his own feast with its place, participants, provider, and food. The second level is either speech or narration (it varies from poem to poem) framed by the first level and concerning the activities of another group or of the same group at different times. In *Le Melon*, for example, the second level is a narration of the Olympian feast of Apollo. *Le Fromage* has internal stories of Apollo's herding of Admetus' cattle and of the rape of Io.

The emphasis on exchange of food that appears in the duplication of this activity on two levels of the text also affects the address of the poems. Many of these texts are explicitly addressed to a benefactor of Saint-Amant. Saint-Amant deals with this social convention of offering thanks by making the exchange between poet and benefactor the theme of the poem itself. The text then is both the object of an exchange and the representation of an exchange. The verse *épître* to the baron de Melay, for example, tells of the addressee's (Melay's) sending of a ham from the Bordeaux region to Paris, where the receiver, the countess of Harcourt, in turn sent it to Saint-Amant's room. The gift is clearly a privilege which belongs traditionally to the aristocracy on which the poet depends; but the poet, as actor in his poem, gets the chance in his turn to play the role of giver by adding to the ham what belongs to the artist—its arrangement or presentation in a higher aesthetic form—by having the ham enclosed in a "palace" made of *pasta*, anchovies, etc., for presentation to another poet, Vauquelin des Yveteaux. The ham, with its accompanying wine (Ciotat) and cheese (Roquefort) are then consumed at Des Yveteaux's house with a number of "revelers" in memory of Melay. The poem's conclusion asks that Melay acknowledge that the poet's work demonstrates his ability to receive and thank properly: "Dy qu'il fait bon me donner quelque chose" (v. 402). This will be a further incitement for giving to Saint-Amant; the poem thus displays and participates in an open-ended process of giving. As a literary text, it can be savored for its verbal qualities (the level of the signifier) of euphony, wit in the selection of words, organization of anecdotes, but it can also be appreciated for its mirroring, in its content, of the activity of the giver.

The way in which the gift is received and consumed is an important part of this exchange. The titles of many of the poems—*La Desbauche, Orgye, La Crevaille*—are enough to indicate their unity in a thematic of excess. Whether the principal object of consumption be wine or food, the activity of what Saint-Amant calls *la débauche*, with its notions of transgression and waste and of defiance of middle-class respect of measure, aims at a kind of collective transcendence of social restraint. The substances that are the object of exchange take on a common property of imparting a kind of intoxication through their use in demonstrating an anti-norm. Excessive consumption alone is not sufficient for a *débauche*; there must also be a community of participants united in consumption of the object given by the *other* community which produces and sells. The particular monetary value of what is gulped down (*briffé*, with connotations close to those of our modern *bouffé*) is displayed in the descriptive metaphors in order to show the complete inversion of commercial values in the anti-norm of the reveler: "en cette Glace arrondie / Brille une lumiere esbaudie, / De la couleur de nos escus" (*Le Cidre*, vv. 4-6). Gold is displayed here not simply as a color, nor even as a precious substance but in the monetary or "fallen" form in which it enters commercial exchange. In *Le Fromage*, the cheese not only looks like gold ("il faroit comparaison / De ce fromage que j'honore /A ce metal que l'homme adore," vv. 74-76) because of its color, but it is also worth much money: "Fromage, que tu vaux d'escus" (v. 14). The speedy and carefree consumption of the *goinfres* is explicitly antithetical to an attitude of measure that respects monetary values: "Chaque morceau vaut un ducat, / Voire six verres de muscat / Et vos dents n'auront point de honte / D'en avoir fait si peu de conte?" (vv. 97-100). One kind of worship is set against another, and one kind of consumption is contrasted with another, the kind which calculates quantitative equivalences. The object—cheese, cider, ham—is the point of contact between two social groups, two activities, and two sets of values.

The presence of the notion of money as it is glimpsed in these comparisons both reveals and conceals the economic status of the speaker and of his benefactors. The food is worth money, but it is not money. It is therefore a gift more than a payment and, by the excessive and aesthetic nature of the gift, any crudeness and humiliation that could be associated with the transfer of money are effaced. This carefree attitude towards the monetary value of the gift raises it to a level of aesthetic object more readily comparable with the gift that the poet will in turn offer his audience. The *débauche* also offers a possibility of inclusion of the addressee within the fictive feast of the poem (e.g., *Epître à de Melay, La Vigne*) and therefore on both sides of the action of exchange, giver and participant in an elite anti-norm.

The source of the object given to the poet provides a metonymic way of praising the poet's benefactor. All of the foods mentioned are from a specific, and of course, non-Parisian place. The ham from the Basque country is a gift from Melay, governor of a castle in Bordeaux. Its excellence reflects on Melay not simply because he is the giver, but because he is by contiguity part of the excellence of the *terroir*. The cider which triumphs over wine in *Le Cidre* is a flattery to its giver and an exaltation of Normandy. The melon cut open by Saint-Amant is better than those from other places and better than other fruits from specific places ("Ny la Poire de Tours sacrée . . ."). The rivalry between places, which, after all, in the seventeenth century was still a contest between aristocracy and monarchy, is the underlying system that gives the metonymic contrast of fruits its meaning.

The food has another metonymic function, however, because of the double origin that it has in most of these poems. Here the second level of the text comes into play, for the internal narration or speech frequently deals with a giving or production of the food by a deity. The mythic characters who replace, while paralleling, the earthly ones in *Le Melon, Le Fromage*, and the *Epître*, provide a new and purely literary place of origin for the gift. The metaphoric level thus enters the text through metonymy. Thus of the Cheese:

> Crois-tu qu'un manger si divin
> Vienne d'une Vache ordinaire?
> Non, non, c'est chose imaginaire.
> Quant à moy je croy qu'il soit fait
> De la quint'essence du lait

Qu'on tira d'Yo transformée
Qui fut d'un Dieu la bien-aymée.
(vv. 110-16)

The Melon, for which an earthly giver is not clearly designated, is taken over by the poem, which refuses to it any earthly origin: "ce MELON divin, / Honneur du Climat Angevin. / Que dis-je, d'Anjou? je m'abuse, / C'est un fruict du crû de ma Muse, / Un fruict en Parnasse eslevé . . ." (vv. 87-91). The earthly topography is overlaid with a literary-mythological one. If, for example, the Melon is first described as "Honneur du climat Angevin" and later as "Un fruict en Parnasse eslevé," then a whole set of potential metaphors are set up on what had been two metonymies of origin. The fruit is then the point of contact between these two topographies and, hence, between two levels of the text, between which we can read such comparisons as Anjou/Parnassus, Melon/ poem.

The food in these various poems as point of contact with the secondary level of the text, as object given by the benefactor to the poet, and as the foundation of the community of the revelers, is made significant only by the poet's words as he performs in the "scene" of the primary level of the text. It is the speaking "I" who makes the food the center of a feast, and it is the "I" who uses the food to define himself, to create his poetic *persona*. The poet's words make the feast and do so by indicating the presence of the food and the other participants or by making a feast out of absences, as Saint-Amant does in *La Vigne*. In this poem the long list of invitations calls into the poem a series of earlier feasts and other places only to designate the poem itself as the feast, the poet as its center, and its tense the indication of what is not, the conditional:

Que n'es-tu maintenant icy!
Nous boirions dedans ta calotte,
Et par quelque chanson falotte
Nous celebrerions la vertu
Qu'on tire de ce bois tortu,
Vray Bilot, Roy de la débauche
Mon cher amy, mon χοϑυλλον gauche,
Si tu te trouvois en ce lieu . . .
(vv. 60-67)

This calling together of interlocutors is a fundamental procedure of Saint-Amant, whose enunciation is profoundly apostrophic. There are many *tu* in *La Vigne*, as there are in *Chanson a boire*, *Le Melon*, and the other texts, and this multiplicity of "receivers" underlines the role of the speaker as nexus of this multiple address. The reader is at first drawn into the text and then distanced from it. Each successive address to a named person makes none of its readers the *tu* of the text. The highly characterized *tu* is both closer to the speaker than is a third person and farther from the reader; it is within the deictic network of the poet's speech, part of the situation which he gives as the instance of his word, and requires *our* absence. We, seeing that we are none of those addressed, retreat from the poem as the poet becomes more strongly present. The effect of enunciation is to characterize the subject, the speaker, against the difference of the person addressed. Saint-Amant's accumulative second person finishes by such a high level of self-characterization that the "I" casts all else into the background.

There are essentially three second persons in Saint-Amant's poems: the rhetorical addressee, the material object, and the mythical figures of the second level. The rhetorical addresses fall into two slightly different categories, that of the benefactor and that of the participants. What could be sharp distinctions between categories—for example, between the apostrophe to the Cheese (animation) and the address to the benefactors—are, by the frequency and multiplicity of changes in the second person, blurred. All becomes present or absent, personified or objectivized, as the poet's word varies. The second persons pass in turn into the third person (e.g., Bilot and the "companions" in *Le Fromage*, the Melon, Apollo), so that in the constant shifting of address only the "I" remains stable.[5]

There is, in the feast itself, a justification for this shifting address. As a "genre," the feast depends on a master of ceremonies, on the one who calls to the others to drink and who directs the significance of their gesture: "Encore un coup donc Compagnons, / Du bon Denys les vrais mignons, / Sus! qu'à plein gosier on s'escrie / Beny soit le terroir de Brie" (*Fromage*, vv. 65-68). It is his word that calls their words or gesture into existence, that gives presence to the myth which, precisely by its mythic quality (its absence), requires celebration for its perpetuation, that makes the name of the benefactor ("un Nom si haut") and of the object appear as the destination of the significant gesture of consumption, in brief, that makes of the meal a feast. In this sense, any feast can have only one voice, the single voice of the master of the feast, which grows out as a synecdoche from the group and attaches itself, in these texts, on an object that is the synecdoche of a region of which it bears the name (Roquefort, Cantal, Brie), and which provides the basis for the metonymic celebrations of divinities and benefactors.

The poems carefully compose the "scene" of the feast around the poet. The *Fromage* begins typically with an indication of the place—"Assis sur le bord d'un chantier / Avec des gens de mon mestier" (*chantier* = platform to hold barrels of wine)—and a designation of the object, the Cheese, and the naming of the giver, Bilot (vv. 1-16). The second level is introduced gradually (vv. 17-40) with a mythification of the place of origin of the Cheese (Brie) through a prayer which raises Brie out of temporal contingency: "Que Flore avec ses beaux atours / Exerçant mille amoureux tours / Sur une immortelle verdure . . ." (vv. 25-27). This leads to a mythic episode in which the poet tells of Mercury's tricking Apollo with Pan's pipes (vv. 41-60). After a modulation in which the poet calls attention to the differences of levels in his text ("Muse, tu vas trop haut"), he returns to the companions and to the first level before moving back to the mythic origins of the Cheese in the story of Io (vv. 113-20). The poem ends with a repetition of the apostrophe to the Cheese and an imperative to the pourer that anchors the text as a whole in the level of the poet's fictive feast. In addition to these two levels, two "scenes," a third meta-discursive function of the poet's reflection on his own speech appears at the joining of the other two levels. The passage from the first level to the second is gradual, a kind of progressive symbolization of the Cheese— as, for instance, when the disappearance of the Cheese is linked to a scholastic contrast between matter and form before the matter itself is raised to the intemporality attributed to the form (vv. 101-20). But the return to the feast, and thus to the consciousness of the poet's word, is highly marked ("Mais cependant que je discours / Ces Goinfres-cy briffent tousjours," vv. 89-90). The reappearance of the feast and of the poet's speech—the latter standing out from the former (*he* talks while *they* eat)—is also a return to the passage of time, while the movement from the first to the second level is towards the intemporal.

Le Cidre would seem to be quite different from *Le Fromage* in its freedom from classical mythology. But it too follows the pattern of localization of the feast (Normandy, the table) and focuses on the glass and its contents (vv. 1-35). The passage into a second level is signaled by the introduction of the name of the benefactor ("à l'honneur du grand SEGUIER") through whom the art of glassmaking will return to the province (vv. 36-60). This passage, dominated by the third person, ends with a return to the first level in much the same way that *Le Fromage* does; the glass of which the fabrication is described in the second level is associated with the glass held by the poet ("ce Vase où rit ce Nectar!"), and the poet points to the distinction between his song and the activity immediately around him: "Mais cependant que je m'amuse / A caqueter de la façon . . ." (vv. 61-62).

The second level is not always a narration. In the *Epître*, the Ham speaks of its own origin in the woods of Diana (vv. 253-92), but here too the change of levels has a meta-discursive function in that the Ham calls on one of those present, a call apparently heeded by the poet, to record its consumption and its difference from ordinary hams. It comes, after all, from a boar hunted by the goddess of the hunt. This discourse, while internally temporal because it has a moment of speaking, points backwards and forwards towards literary immortality. Yet the return to the primary level of the text is a reminder of the non-existence of this speech in the time of the feast itself, for it was spoken by "Le bon muet" and "heard" with the tongue.

The object exchanged and consumed is, if not the poem's center, certainly the major point of contact between the poet and his addressees. The substances that constitute this object in the various poems bring to the text qualities of their own. The innocuous edibles of Saint-Amant's poems deserve a closer look. *Cucuminis melo* may be the same today as it was in the 1600s in terms of bio-genetic descendance, but the conception of even the most common object is influenced by the movement of language; the reference may be the same, but what is signified differs. In this sense, the melon of Saint-Amant was not the same as ours. In the seventeenth century, the melon could kill. Jacques Pons, medical doctor to Henri IV and author of a *Traité du melon*, points to the illustrious victims of melons and shows not only medical but moral reprobation: "Il y a eu des Papes, des Empereurs et des Roys qui en sont morts, et qui ont payé bien cher un plaisir leger & d'une courte durée."⁶ The victims include Pope Paul II, the Emperors Albert, Frederic III, and Henry VII. Was the melon responsible for these deaths? It matters little, for the melon, as semantic entity, consists of what is said about it, what has been called the "propos sur le monde" or "le radotage."⁷ The melon, in this anonymous babbling, is the fruit of predilection of the libertine, of the reveler. The eater of melons weighs, as Pons says, a fleeting pleasure against eternity and chooses the instant. But more than that, he chooses a *way* of eating. In instructing his readers to eat melons safely ("Des moyens d'user du Melon sans en estre offensé"), Pons reports the general opinion that the melon eater should drink wine. Melons lead to wine; many melons require much wine. The fruit is the accompaniment and the excuse for drinking, and Pons claims that this "medical" reasoning was, in fact, abused: "On en sert des piramides et des montagnes . . . on s'en creve le soir, à midy, le matin, et à toute heure, c'est l'unique employ des illustres débauchez . . . on boit à proportion avec cette pensée mortelle et peu raisonnable que le vin pur digere ce fruit, et qu'il en empesche la corruption . . ." (p. 37). Not only wine, but good, mature wine, according to other authors on plants: "que ceux qui sont phlegmatiques boivent apres de quelque bon vin vieil."⁸

This emblem of the libertine feast, which had already been the subject of a French poem of the length of Saint-Amant's, Martial Le Maistre's *Procès du Melon* (Paris: 1607),⁹ is like the cheeses and the hams because they all invite drinking and excess. The Cantal, which is described in such apparently negative terms— "Gousset, écafignon, faguenas, camboüis" (or the smell of the armpit, of the feet, of rot, and of goat grease)—has supreme value because of the explicit link between it and wine. It creates an unquenchable thirst, the kind that furnishes the open-ended perspective that is such an important part of these cultic poems: "Au secours Sommelier, j'ay la luëtte en feu, / Je brusle dans le corps, parbieu! ce n'est pas jeu; / Des brocs, des seaux de vin pour tascher de l'esteindre, / Verse eternellement, il ne faut point se feindre" (vv. 69-72). This affinity extends, though with less intensity, to the triad Ciotat wine, Roquefort, and Bayonne ham of the *Epître* ("Que leur vertu s'accorde, et se ressemble," v. 242).

The properties frequently associated with the object are only the somewhat crude and preliminary basis for the poet's *use* of the object in his language and his action. The poet can uncover properties less often associated with the object and can confer new properties, or at least new functions and valuations, by his way of designating it. In these poems, Saint-Amant designates his objects as sacred both in pagan mythic terms and in Christian terms. The divine (pagan and literary) origin proposed is one form of this special valuation of the food, but the feast itself provides analogies, carefully used by Saint-Amant, with the Christian eucharist.

To a thoroughly modern reader of French and Christian background, eating is rarely associated with notions of powerful prohibition. Eating is not expected to have any effect on a soul nor on the social freedom and position of the consumer. At the very most, food has a symbolic function extending no further than the indication of mood, political consciousness (boycotts of various products), or social class (the *gourmet*, well traveled and cosmopolitan). Food, in other words, is neither sacramental nor sinful. For Saint-Amant's time, food was potentially both of these things, and the poet frequently reminds us of the rules weighing on our tables: "si les Oeufs ne sont pas assez frais à ton gré, pour estre mangez en coque, fais-en des Aumelettes: Le Fromage et le Jambon avec quoy l'on en faict d'excellentes ne te manqueront point en ce lieu; & combien que ce soit en Caresme, tu en pourras manger sans dispense, si ce n'est qu'il en faille avoir pour les yeux & pour les oreilles a qui se destinent ces viandes-là" ("au lecteur," 2e partie, II, 95). With customary wit,

Saint-Amant points out the ecclesiastical censorship that affected both the mental and physical appetites of seventeenth-century France. In *Les Nobles triolets* he returns to the notion of imposed fasting in mentioning the suspension of the Lenten rules during the siege of Paris in 1649: "Puis qu'il n'est point de Mardy-gras / Il ne sera point de Caresme; / Je n'en feray jour en mes dras / Puis qu'il n'est point de Mardy-gras; / Je veux me refaire le bras / En deust crever le Jeusne mesme, / Puis qu'il n'est point de Mardy-gras / Il ne sera point de Caresme" (vv. 17-24).

The sacred can be defined in general as that which is forbidden, that which is untouchable because it has been "set apart," usually for offering to a divinity. The notion of the sacred is thus connected with transgression, just as Lent and Carnival are inseparable, since normal rules are suspended in regard to the sacred: normally the destruction or waste of food is forbidden, but its destruction is obligatory once it has been "set aside" for the gods.[10] Saint-Amant calls upon the notions of excess and transgression in many of the cultic poems, as, for example, in *Le Cidre*:

> Ha! que ce bruit m'est agreable!
> Voylà respondu comme il faut;
> J'en esprouve un aise incroyable,
> Et nostre Desbauche est loüable
> D'esclater pour un Nom si haut:
> Aux graces qu'on desire en elle
> La retenuë est criminelle,
> La froideur offence Themis,
> Bref, pour la rendre solennelle
> L'excez mesme nous est permis.
> (vv. 71-80)

Here the conditions of a sacrifice are fulfilled. Under the guidance of the speaker, the many participants are called upon to respond with the appropriate gesture (the raising of the cups, v. 68); the activity is centered on the praise of "un Nom si haut," normal constraints on drinking are completely reversed and the ordinary conduct becomes "criminal." Finally, the name of a divinity—though not the destination of the sacrifice—is given with the mention of Themis, goddess of custom and righteousness.

In the *Epître* for de Melay the twin notions of the forbidden and the sacrificial are both made explicit. The ham, enclosed in

its miniature palace "en Roy," is described as the food that distinguishes good Christians from Jews and Moslems: "Ce digne
Mets, qui des Mets tient le trosne, / Et par qui seul, les Juifs
estant morguez, / Les bons Chrestiens des Turcs sont distinguez"
(vv. 190-92). The meat, prohibited by dietary laws (later in the
text Saint-Amant mentions the Coranic prohibition of wine), is
necessarily eaten by good Christians. Thus, even though ham is
shown to be eminently permissible, even necessary (a *necessary
transgression*), the concept of sin is established in the background,
the law followed by the participants in the feast is set in contrast
to the law of another group, and the meat is given symbolic as
well as alimentary importance. The ham, after being placed in
the new container ordered by the poet, is transferred to the
home of the poet-character Des Yveteaux in a eucharistic procession ("Je fis marcher en pas de Pain benit / Ce Don Royal
que de fleurs on garnit," vv. 215-16) and consumed in a "Sacrifice" during which the poet imagines the ham to speak to those
who sacrifice and consume it:

> Chers Ennemis, je beny mes blessures,
> Je suis heureux d'esprouver vos morsures,
> Puis que le Sort m'ordonne noblement
> De vous servir d'agreable aliment;
> Ma chair de beste en chair d'homme changée,
> Sera tantost à vos dents obligée . . .
>   (vv. 253-58)

The notions of the happy victim, blessing its wounds, alluding to
the supernatural order that causes its end and evoking the transformation of its flesh, are part of this only slightly veiled eucharistic level of the text, a characteristic that was noted with severity
in the seventeenth century.[11] Further, the victim charges one of
those present to write the story of the ham so that its relation to
divinity can be known: "non point comme un morceau / Qui
soit venu d'un vulgaire Pourceau, / Mais, pour certain, comme
l'enorme fesse / D'un grand Sanglier que Diane confesse / Avoir
esté la terreur de ses Bois" (vv. 267-71). This origin, again replacing, halfway through the poem, a referential with a purely literary
source, is doubly significant, for it links its literary transformation into a sacred object (Diana, etc.) to the aristocratic rank of

its giver (the hunt, as opposed to pig raising, being a privilege of the nobility).

The vessel in which the object is transported and from which it is consumed is also a means of sacralization, though the process moves in two directions, the vessel becoming valued for what it contains, while the object contained is set apart from others of its class by its container. This is clearly the case for the ham, but it is most remarkable in *Le Cidre*, where this reciprocal valorization is more important. The glass from which the poet drinks cider, the *or potable*, is emphasized by its appearance at the line end rhyme, in internal rhyme ("je le revere"), in synonymy (*cristal*, with its additional connotations of rarity and worth), and by the description, in two strophes, of its fabrication and social significance. It is the "plus noble effort du feu," and "Art de Prince," and causes "Miracles" of transformation, of substance. The vessels made from it are ennobled by their contact with the king ("maint Ouvrage superbe / Y prétend aux lévres d'un Roy," vv. 49-50), a continuation of the metonymic procedure by which meaning is created through contiguity. The nobility of the substance is also a result of the restriction of its manufacture in France to a special caste, the "noblesse de verre" still privileged in the exercise of the Art of Fire (hence the "Art de Prince"). The strophes describing glassmaking accentuate the interplay between the human and the inanimate in such a way that the glass is formed by the constituent quality of life (*anima*, breath): "Quand animé d'un souffle humain, / Un Prodige en délicatesse / S'enfle, et se forme avec justesse" (vv. 52-54). The content of the glass is thus set apart from drink by the valorization of its container and vice versa, an ambivalence that is part of this poem because of its destination, for the text is a celebration of (and an expression of thanks for) both hospitality—the count de Brionne—and the privilege of glassmaking—Séguier.

Finally, the sacralization of the object offered and consumed is achieved through a gradual accumulation of words bearing the concept of religion, pagan or Christian, and by syntactic configurations that are characteristic of liturgical language, such as the forty-four verse litany to Bacchus in *La Desbauche*: "Par ton sainct portrait que j'esbauche / . . . / Par ta couronne de Lierre,

/ Par la spendeur de ce grand verre, / Par ton Thirse tant redouté
... ," etc. (vv. 35-78). In *Le Fromage* there is a kind of doxology
accompanied by liturgical gesture as directed by the speaker: "A
genoux Enfans desbauchez, / Chers confidents de mes pechez, /
Sus! qu'à plein gosier on s'escrie / Beny soit le terroir de Brie, /
Beny soit son plaisant aspect . . ." (vv. 17-21). In the *Epître*
there is, mixed into the eucharistic procession, a kind of pagan
libation (v. 239).

All that we have seen points to the figurative equivalence established between poetry and food and drink, or, rather, to several
equivalences that center on the ostensible consumption of an
object to create a rich network of comparisons and metaphor.
The most fundamental, the one that joins the primary and
secondary levels, is the replacement of the "literal" food by the
literary one. In *Le Melon* this substitution permits a potential
literary-historical correction as well as a rhetorical one (vv. 87-
100); by replacing the Angevin fruit with one of his own Muse,
Saint-Amant is asserting his own poetic invention against the
great singers of the fruit and wine of Anjou and the Loire, both
praising the fruit of Tours and Anjou as the best that earth has
to offer and then going one step beyond to the Parnassus of
his own personal creation. The Muse links the poet to Parnassus,
where the geographical explanation becomes a metaphoric one.
The fruit grows better when it is closer to the sun (Apollo), god
of poetry. The notion of place is doubled by its meaning in
spatial terms (*lieu commun*, everyday, terrestrial place), and in
rhetoric (*lieu commun*, commonplace). In *Le Melon* there is no
benefactor who gives the poet his fruit in the primary level, so
that the poet is not rivaling a benefactor, but, by removing the
apparent referential support that the poem has up to this point
(where Saint-Amant seems to be describing a real melon), the
poet places himself in parallel with Apollo himself, who is the
giver of the melon in the internal narrative.

In *Le Fromage* (quoted above), the apparently literal origin
of the cheese is questioned by the multivocal "Non, non, c'est
chose imaginaire," with its play between the antecedence of this
chose. Is it the revelers' belief in the earthly production of the
cheese, or is it the *manger divin* itself which is imaginary? This

replacement of an origin—which is also a re-placement, since it calls into being a new topography—is a transformation of the object that the poet does not hesitate to motivate or emphasize. In the case of the cheese, the object which the poet transforms by designating it verbally as different is the product of a mythic metamorphosis and fecundation. Furthermore, the resulting, and literary, milk is a *quintessence*. Consequently, it is not only pure, but associated with the mysterious transformations of alchemy and with the Rabelaisian tradition (both alchemy and Pantagruel figure in cultic texts of Saint-Amant).[12] Thus the origin of the cheese recedes ever deeper into the literary imagination. But the text recalls quickly the physical appearance of the object (v. 120) by pointing to its apparent age to justify the metaphoric origin. This is another case of poetic motivation—the poet extends his concept so that more and more elements of the text are explained by it, so that less is left to "chance"—but also a reminder that the "reality" of the poem proceeds from the figurative to the literal and not in the opposite direction. All is justified in terms of the literary-mythic transformation.

The alchemical potable gold of *Le Cidre* and the transformation of the flesh in the *Epître* (where the context authorizes the term transubstantiation) permit us to see that there are a number of traditions (represented by codes of significant individual words or of syntactic groupings) that work on the basis of certain shared concepts. The allusions to alchemy, to liturgy, and to metamorphosis (e.g., the stories of Io and of the origin of the flute in *Le Fromage*, the origin of the lute in *Le Melon*) converge on the theme of transformation. This is indeed the function of the cultic feast, where ordinary objects are, as we have seen, transformed by the speaker's act of *naming*; the object remains, in the poet's presentation of the first level, the same—the cheese looks just as it did before, aged and yellow—but the visible characteristics become the guarantee of qualities entirely linguistic in origin, its mythic origin in Jupiter's love.[13] Transformation, but a metaphoric and invisible one, is the function of the eucharistic liturgy that appears and disappears in the *Epître*; it is the function of alchemy, of literary metamorphosis, and of the Rabelaisian quintessence, marrow, and bottle (themselves determined in part by alchemical and liturgical forms).

Two of these codes also include the twin notions of memory (or memorialization) and of origin. The stories of metamorphosis as they appear in mythology and as they are assembled by Ovid, to whom Saint-Amant was so much indebted, are stories of the origin of the world and of the texts around us. The liturgy founds a "new and everlasting covenant" and represents the origin of a new substance, the sacrificial body of Christ. The feasts in which the objects of Saint-Amant's texts are consumed also unite memory and origin, and do so with numerous branchings. They record the gift of an object on the primary level—the Brie from Bilot, the ham from Melay, the cantal from the "Franc et noble Marquis [de Mortemart]," the cider from Brionne, the glass-making patent from Séguier—and promise the memorialization of the donor and of the metonymic object. The same poems inscribe in the secondary level the origin of the object consumed and of the poetic or musical tradition. *Le Fromage*, for example, contains two representations of mythic cattle into one of which is written the Apollonian song and origin of the rustic pipes and into the other the origin of the milk in Io. In the first of these sections of *Le Fromage*, the poet moves from a praise of the cheese to a praise of the place of its production (Brie) to a prayer that it be visited by Apollo who could watch the cheese-producing cows, but more carefully than he watched the herd of Admetus:

> Lors que le Patron des Mattois
> Portant cinq crocs au lieu de dolts,
> Qui faisoient le saut de la carpe,
> Joüa sur ses bœufs de la harpe,
> Et le laissa sous un Ormeau
> Fluster son soul d'un chalumeau,
> Que jadis l'amoureux martyre
> Fit entonner au grand Satyre.
> (vv. 45-52)

This story, which itself has the allegoric meaning of Apollo's passing from his cithar to the humbler pastoral song of the pipe, points towards the humbleness (though certainly not humility) of Saint-Amant's own song—several verses later he interrupts his narrative digression to accuse himself of moving in the opposite direction ("Muse, tu vas trop haut")—and associates the source of the milk and cheese with the divine origin of the pastoral and epic songs. The next mention of milk and cows occurs with the story of Io, made into a cow in a metamorphosis that is parallel to that of Syrinx into a reed. The attribution of the cheese of the poem to Io (through the medium of the poet whose presence is accentuated at every passage from level to level: "Quant a moy je croy qu'il soit fait . . .") thus closes the circle of transformation within which both pastoral poetry and the cheese find their origin.

These poems are metaphorically open-ended. Not only do the two levels allude to one another in such a way that the literal and symbolic fruit refer constantly back to each other, but the activities of the feast are self-perpetuating. Memory provokes drinking, as do the melon, the ham, and the cantal. As long as there is one, there will be the other. The gesture of the *toppe*, raising the cup or glass, calls for the name that gives it a meaning:

> Et que ce grand mot d'*A Boire*,
> Mette tant de pots a sec,
> Qu'une eternelle memoire
> S'en puisse exercer le bec.
> (*La Crevaille*, vv. 22-25)

Likewise the memory of the benefactor calls for the gesture of honor. The parallel of the annual planting of melons and the fruitfulness of the poet's Muse ("Sur un Ciron un Livre elle feroit," *Epître*, v. 384) is part of the basic structure of all the cultic poems, many of which add to this semantic opening a metric or formal one as well. *Le Fromage*, after a repetition of verses 13-16, ends with the imperative "VERSE LAQUAIS," so that in metric terms the closure of the last verse and of the verse form itself is negated, while at the same time the semantic motif of presentation-consumption is broken and left incomplete, soliciting the reader to supply the missing movement.[14] Similarly, the "Chanson à boire" finishes with an extrastrophic "VIVAT." Endings of this type (which appear only in the poems from before 1629) seem to have a literary connotation as well, suggested by "La Naissance de Pantagruel," which concludes "Si bien qu'à mon exemple, ainsi que dit l'histoire, / Par tout à gueule ouverte on demandoit à boire. / A BOIRE, A BOIRE." Saint-Amant seems to accept here the metaphorics of the earlier textual tradition.

The stress on the duration of the actions of drinking and toasting, and on the eternal presence of the name of the cultic object in the works of the poet ("les cahiers du bon gros SAINT-AMANT," *Le Melon*), finally places the poet in a position of superiority in the exchange with his benefactor. The object given by the patron is consumed, as in *Le Fromage*:

> Bilot, qui m'en avois muny,
> Hé! pourquoy n'est-il infiny
> Tout aussi bien en sa matiere
> Qu'il l'estoit en sa forme entiere?
> Pourquoy tousjours s'apetissant,
> De Lune devient-il Croissant?
> Et pourquoy si bas sous la nuë
> S'éclipse-t-il a nostre veuë?
> (vv. 101-08)

The poet's reproachful question provides the argument for the poet's action, for the eclipse of Bilot's Brie coincides with the gradual unfolding of Saint-Amant's *Fromage*. The eternity of the circle figured in the cheese is the ultimate metaphor for the poet's act. The cheese disappears, its circle stays. The melon is consumed, but the writing that covers it—and Saint-Amant's laughter—remains.

Let us cut more deeply into Saint-Amant's *Melon*, the most celebrated of his cultic poems. A rapid description of the poem's unfolding shows that it depends on an alternance of suspense and revelation.[15] It begins with a localization of the action around the speaking *Je* and with a focusing on an object, as yet unnamed, but already suggested by its sensory characteristics ("Quelle odeur sens-je en cette Chambre?" v. 1), from which the poet empties possible causes to create a suspense ("A-t-on bruslé de la pastille? / N'est-ce point ce vin qui petille / . . . / Non, ce n'est rien d'entre ces choses, / Mon penser, que tu me proposes . . .," vv. 9, 10, 17). A tension is created between what is given as a (fictive) referential dimension and the linguistic dimensions—the mind's *proposing* of objects to the poet—which will eventually introduce the object into the text. The void thus created heightens the value of the Melon when it is named (v. 21). A second sequence of negative description by elimination of various comparable fruits (vv. 69-89) leads to the introduction of the second level of the poem, the narrative of the Olympian feast, by again creating a void that calls for the revelation of the divine original melon. A brief return to the first level provides a transition towards the long second-level narration by showing how this narration relates to the fruit, the god, and the companions at the feast. Addressing Apollo, the poet promises to "Dire en ce lieu ce que je pense, / Et de ce MELON, et de toy, / Suivant les signes que j'en voy" (vv. 110-12). This second level ends with the poet's pointing towards himself and to his song (v. 297) when he has filled his promise to tell a story. He returns briefly to the second level (vv. 305-08) to link the melon of the Olympians to the melon on the table and finishes in the first level by an address to the melon that opens the end of the poem towards perpetuity. Saint-Amant does this by a series of impossible things (*adynata* in classical rhetoric) that will have to come to pass before the effacement of the melon from the poet's writing ("Avant que je t'oublie, et que ton goust charmant / Soit biffé des Cahiers du bon gros SAINT-AMANT").

On the primary level, the human feast, there are three principal moments of suspense: before the discovery of the fruit, before the revelation of the divine origin, and at the conclusion, in which the suspense of the accumulated impossibilities that form a single sentence is relieved only in the subordinate clause of the last two verses. Each case of suspense involves the discovery of an identity, of a name: the MELON, Parnassus and Olympus, and SAINT-AMANT. The process of successive revelations leads to the "signature" of the poet himself after designating, at the principal articulations of the poem, the other objects which are figures of the poet and his text.

The first of these discoveries, the melon, has an apparent metaphorical intention. The characteristic attributed to the melon immediately upon its discovery is the form of the markings on its skin:

C'est un MELON, où la Nature,
Par une admirable structure,
A voulu graver à l'entour
Mille plaisans chiffres d'Amour,
Pour claire marque à tout le monde,

Que d'une amitié sans seconde
Elle cherit ce doux manger.
(vv. 21-27)

The second discovery, the fruit's origin, introduces the story of
the Olympian banquet (vv. 117-296) in which Phoebus, "Dieu
des Fruicts, et des Vers" (v. 104), brought the melon which far
surpassed the other things eaten:

Il ne se treuva rien à l'égal d'un MELON
Que Thalie apporte pour son maistre Apollon.
Que ne fut-il point dit en celebrant sa gloire?
Et que ne diroit-on encore à sa memoire?
Le Temps qui frippe tout, ce Gourmand immortel,
Jure n'avoir rien veu, ny rien mangé de tel . . .
(vv. 255-60)

This discovery, which, in the poem's fictive chronology, precedes
the discovery of the poet more than two hundred verses before,
opens a series of temporal conceits. The melon was brought to
the banquet for Apollo by Thalia, the muse of Comedy, whose
mother, Mnemosyne, was goddess of memory. The poet's text is
part of a fictive tradition of memorials to this melon, a tradition
of which he emphasizes the opening into the future. Time himself, Cronos, who eats his children, the hours,[16] here eats the
melon, but without destroying it, for the melon is outside of
time, especially if the wordplay of Saint-Amant is permitted its
usual freedom: "Le Temps . . . / Jure n'avoir rien veu, ny rien
mangé de tel." Time never ate anything as good as this melon;
Time never ate "any such thing." The melon is thus the gift of
one of the daughters of memory, is preserved in memory by
language, is consumed by time but survives. But the melon also
becomes the origin of the musical instrument that permits the
perpetuation of the kind of language in which it is praised.
Apollo, at the end of the feast, makes of it the first lute. This
story of the origin of the lute again opposed the deities, who are
at the origin of musical instruments in *Le Fromage*:

Phoebus qui le tenoit, sentant sa fantaisie
D'un desir curieux en cét instant saisie,
En coupe la moitié, la creuse proprement;
Bref pour finir le conte, en fait un Instrument,
Dont la forme destruit et renverse la Fable

De ce qu'on a chanté, que jadis sur le sable
Mercure trouvant mort un certain Limaçon,
Qui vit parfois en beste, et parfois en poisson,
Soudain en ramassa la Cocque harmonieuse,
Avec quoy, d'une main aux Arts ingenieuse,
Aussi bien qu'aux Larcins, tout à l'heure qu'il eut,
Au bord d'une Riviere il fit le premier Lut.
(vv. 273-84)

The melon, by being consumed, provides the material for the fabrication of the lute. Saint-Amant not only provides a myth of origin for the lute, he does so by explicitly substituting a new version (much could be said about the *burlesque*, to which this poem belongs, as the art of substitution).[17] The acute literary consciousness of Saint-Amant as author of a poem about the origin of poetry is underlined by his insistence on giving both the new version and the old version side-by-side. He provides the key term of *reversal* for what he is doing and shows how his creation grows out of literary reversal, just as the kind of feast that appears in the cultic poems generally is based on a social reversal. And, if any reader might have missed the passage from the story of the origin of the melon to the origin of song, the poet describes the latter as "Plus doux que le manger qu'on en avoit tiré."

There is, in each of the mentions of the melon in this text, a gradual displacement—linear and successive—from the consumable melon and its sharing towards the song produced about the production of song. The poet in this way signifies the final subject of his poem, sharing of memory through song, both metonymically, by this linear movement, and metaphorically, by the relationships established between his poem and the melon earlier in the poem (v. 90) and later by the sustained metaphor that results from the presence of the primary and secondary levels. Towards the end of the poem, these two levels are linked by the fiction of the descent of Saint-Amant's edible melon from Apollo's:

... je croy que ce fruict, qui possede nos yeux,
Provient de celuy-là que brifferent les Dieux:
Car le Roy d'Helicon, le Demon de ma veine,
Dans le coin d'un mouchoir en garda de la graine,
Afin que tous les Ans il en pust replanter,
Et d'un soin liberal nous en faire gouster.
(vv. 303-08)

The two functions of god of fruits and god of poetic inspiration are linked in Apollo once more, and the perpetuation of memory is paralleled by the seasonal planting and harvesting of melons. The metaphoric working of the poem is thus assured by a super-imposition of two feasts, two discoveries, two songs, two singers, and, most of all, two melons. The relationships from one level to the other are based on comparisons of the type: Saint-Amant is to the human feast what Apollo is to the mythic feast, the "literal" melon is to Saint-Amant what the mythic melon is to Apollo, etc. The link between the two levels is reinforced and complicated by the descendence of the first from the second level, the kind of fiction of origin seen in *Le Fromage*, and a dominance, as well, of the figurative over the literal that guides us towards a non-gastronomic reading of the text. The back-and-forth movement between the two levels is quickened by the burlesque nature of Saint-Amant's language, an accentuation, to the absurd, of the anthropomorphism of the pagan gods by a refusal to observe linguistic register (or poetic "decorum").

The mock-heroic feasts are one way of evoking the poetic act, a way of absorbing time and text into a centripetal aesthetic object.[18] There is a circularity to this conception of poetry (a pun of Saint-Amant's invention, in his round cheeses and melons), and its withdrawal of senses from the poet, who confounds all in one at the beginning of *Le Melon*, is an apt metaphor for the exclusive concentration on the act of transmission and reception of the poetic object. Saint-Amant was acutely conscious, however, of another problem of the poet in the Late Renaissance: the relationship of aesthetic and memorializing language to heroic event. In a large group of poems, Saint-Amant extends the range of his reflections on poetry to include the "matter" of literature as it is born out of a contest between different conceptions of historical reality and its communication.

Chapter III

HEROIC EVENTS

As the author of what has been called the only work "to escape even partially" the "common disaster" of the epic in seventeenth-century France, Saint-Amant deserves our attention for his way of presenting the kind of heroic events on which epic and several other poetic genres are based.[1] Modern readers of Saint-Amant's first heroic idyll, *Moÿse sauvé*—a group of scholars that as a whole does not coincide with the group interested in Saint-Amant's lyric poetry—have moved away from Boileau's condemnation of the poet whose accomplishment it was "d'une voix insolente, / Chanter du peuple hébreu la fuite triomphante."[2] Instead, attaching less importance to the insolence or personal unworthiness of the poet, they have found in the preface and text of *Moÿse sauvé* a subtle and successful attempt to convey in narrative a biblical event which would seem to lend itself with difficulty to heroic treatment.

The *Moÿse sauvé* is, however, only one of two heroic idylls. The second, *La Généreuse* (1658), offers a chance to explore Saint-Amant's rhetorical strategy as it is applied to a contemporary event. In reading *La Généreuse*, it is important to see it as part of a large group of texts about achievements of the nobility. This is a strange collection of works and the reader, even before passing the title page or dedication, wonders at the odd choice of subjects. There seems to be a fascination with the fleeting or eccentric event. In addition to *La Généreuse*, which treats an event in the Polish and Swedish conflict, there are *L'Albion* (about the English parliamentary wars), *Les Pourveus bachiques* (with references to various current military campaigns), *L'Epistre héroï-comique*, addressed to Gaston d'Orléans on the subject of the siege of Gravelines, and *Le Passage de Gibraltar*, a *caprice héroï-comique* about the naval campaign in the Mediterranean in 1636-37. They contain, or are largely composed of, references to events sometimes widely known and quickly forgotten, sometimes only vaguely understood in France, and sometimes simply expected but never realized. Biographical accident and the desire for patronage can explain some of the choices of subject, but not Saint-Amant's deliberate emphasis on the transitory nature of these events and on the difficulty they offered the reader of the poems. In the "au lecteur" to *La Généreuse* he writes, "il arrive que ce qui estoit bon à dire en une saison ne l'estant plus en une autre, l'esprit se trouve d'abord embarrassé à le comprendre, sans l'avertissement que je dis."[3] But the lapse of time between event and text is not new with Saint-Amant; it is a permanent condition of historical poetry.[4] Furthermore, the craft of the heroic poet has generally included techniques of exposition for closing the gap between the knowledge of the reader and the background necessary for understanding the plot. Saint-Amant, instead of smoothing the reader's way into the events recounted in the poem, insists in his prefaces and other external commentary and in the poems themselves on the difficulties and gaps between the event and the writing of the poem and between the terms of the poem and the knowledge of the public, going so far as to annotate his texts when they contain "quelques termes que les plus Doctes ne sçavent pas, ny ne sont pas mesme obligez de sçavoir."[5] If Saint-Amant's poetry contains such difficulties, they can be attributed only to Saint-Amant's own choice of what to use as the subject of his compositions (their matter), of how to place the speaker in time and space and of the degree to which the text will draw the reader's attention away from the occurrence of the event itself.

La Généreuse, less often studied than the *Moÿse sauvé* of five years before, is linked to the first heroic idyll by the fact that the audience of the *Moÿse sauvé*, the Queen of Poland, is the subject of *La Généreuse*. This fairly long text (1,026 verses in 114 strophes) can be divided, for a first approximation, into three sections: first, the opening statement or "scene of the poet" (strophes 1-7); second, a long account of the events in Warsaw during two days of the war between the Polish and Swedish armies during the summer of 1656, and the departure of the Queen from Warsaw (strophes 8-110); and finally, a statement of the relationship between human activity (event and language) and God (strophes 111-14).

The title of the poem already indicates a somewhat unconventional feature. It is focused on the Queen, Louise-Marie, daughter of the Duc de Nevers, rather than on the King of Poland, Casimir, whose actions seem to be much less successful than those of his Queen. The Queen spends the day in the palace and a garden on one side of the Vistula, while Casimir commands the troops on the battlefield on the other side of the river. Casimir would be the more immediately apparent center for the poem. The text, therefore, is evidently an oblique or decentered presentation of what conventional military history or epic would present as the "event" of note.

This view of the event can be explained on historical and economic grounds; Saint-Amant was, at one time, the secretary of the Queen of Poland, and *La Généreuse* is dedicated to the Princess Palatine, her sister. But these justifications for the way of recounting this battle do not reduce the importance of this decentered viewpoint in Saint-Amant's general practice. This is only one of many texts, as we shall see, that remove speaker from event. Furthermore, the repeated instances of indirection in the presentation of this event make it apparent that Saint-Amant chose to base the text as a whole on the play between presence and absence, and on the indirect manifestation of event or process. There is something decidedly unhistorical about this text, since this indirect presentation runs counter to the objective character of history as defined by modern theoreticians. If "history" (*histoire*) is a model in which "no one is speaking," then

Saint-Amant's "stories" are emphatically discursive, for in them everyone (to exaggerate only slightly) is speaking. The result of this plurality of voices is a distance between the speaker and the content of his speech, but a distance that in no way assures objectivity.[6]

This distance is created for the poem as a whole in the opening section, the "scene of the poet," that is familiar to all readers of Saint-Amant (e.g., *La Solitude*). Here the scene in the woods does not claim the absolute character of the retreat in *La Solitude*, which has no apparent epic or political dimension, for the scene in *La Généreuse* is defined at once as being contemporary with, but distant from, the specific military events that are part of the matter of the poem. At the moment of the Queen's resistance to the outrages of fortune, elsewhere the poet is composing tranquilly:

> Jamais Retraite solitaire
> Ne fut plus propre à mon loisir;
> Jamais je n'en pouvois chosir
> Qui pour mon Luth sçeust mieux se taire.
> Tout ayde à mon dessein, tout en cette Saison,
> Si muable en sa liaison,
> Sert à m'en ébaucher l'Idée:
> Elle est rude, elle est belle, et mesme est secondée
> Par l'assiette de la Maison.
>
> (vv. 10-18)

The notions of time and space, as they affect the poet's ability to tell the events, reappear throughout the poem. In the strophes that follow the evocation of this scene and in which Warsaw gradually replaces the garden and woods, the poet substitutes spatial coincidence/temporal absence for temporal coincidence/spatial absence, recalling his stay in Warsaw at a moment in the past ("Ah! quand je viens a me repeindre / Le lustre ou j'ay veu cet Estat," vv. 73-74, where the temporal difference appears not only in the tense, but in the choice of *repeindre*). The passage in which the two principal characters of the poem, Louise and Casimir, are presented together is another occasion for emphasis on the distance of the poet from his object and the purely imaginary and fictive nature of his account:

Dieu! quelle bouche pourroit dire
L'accueil de ces grands Demy-Dieux?
Hé! que l'absence de leurs yeux
Cache de choses à ma Lyre!
Il faut qu'on s'imagine et de voir, et d'oüir
Tout ce qui peut les réjoüir
En des façons tendres et graves,
Et sçachant leurs projets et resolus et braves,
Du futur mesme il faut joüir.

                          (strophe 18, vv. 154-62)

This strophe introduces a section (strophes 19-31) in which the poet carries out his own injunction.

Before the account of the battle, there is a similar intervention in which the conventional form of an address to the Muse serves to introduce a serious problem of heroic poetry in the modern age, the transient and fragmentary nature of ordinary information and its conflict with the formal and temporal demands of heroic poetry. The poet's project is profoundly linked to the possibility of duration. He is creating something that will last for ages; this is the value of his poetry to those who were celebrated in it—the writer's promise to make their deeds meaningful by transmitting them to posterity. But the speaker's presentation of himself as absent from the scene of the events he is telling makes his own account suspect:

Muse, qu'allons-nous entreprendre?
A peine en sommes-nous instruits;
Et cependant, sur quelques bruits,
Aux Aages nous voulons l'apprendre:
Encore la pluspart de ces bruits passagers
Sont et si vains et si legers
Qu'on n'y peut donner de creance;
Et souvent, aprés tout, la seule bien-seance
Fait les vrais et les mensongers.

                          (vv. 316-24)

Saint-Amant apparently gathered most of his anecdotes for *La Généreuse* from *La Gazette*, and in other poems like *Les Pourveus bachiques* his dependence on this journal for his material is made explicit.[7] But Saint-Amant's finding information in *La Gazette* and his incorporation of other media (the oral "gazette" of the Pont-Neuf) is not as relevant as his *revealing* this textual background. Nothing, after all, obliged him to do so, and poets would continue to write heroic poetry in the era of "modern" communications without displaying the difference between their text and that of general information. The question to the Muse is, in fact, a rhetorical question in the fullest sense. It poses a problem of rhetoric while at the same time it alters the mode of presentation of the whole event. While apparently undermining the veracity of its statement, the strophe continues by undermining the standards by which poetry can be judged through confrontation with the "factual" or referential texts on which our ordinary conception of the political and military event are based. Such texts are only "bruits passagers." Furthermore, as the poet indicates in the following strophes, he has already provided himself with an excuse by emphasizing his absence: "Et si tu manques en leurs traits / L'absence t'en sera l'excuse" (vv. 327-28). The image of the absent poet is therefore a mechanism by which fiction can be justified, but his absence also maintains a thematic of the problem of knowledge later decisively stated as the superiority of a certain reading of event over a simple reporting of it.

The heavy underlining of transitions in the telling of events in Warsaw serves to bring out the distance between the speaker and the object. This is the case, for example, of the attribution of problems of perception to a source within the distant scene of battle. The battle becomes so furious that the smoke "s'esleve de telle sorte / Que mon œil n'y connoist plus rien; / Tout m'est caché, mais aussi bien / Ma veine en autre lieu me porte" (vv. 658-61).

These indications of the speaker's absence and of the separation between him and what he is describing are only the first or most external level of the text's narrative distance. The poem also abounds in internal speakers and listeners, so that the functions of telling and witnessing seem to be coming from within the text rather than from the poet. The categories of listener and speaker are closely, and ironically, intertwined. When the poet sets forth the conversation between Louise and Casimir, a discourse of which he has just emphasized the purely imaginary nature, he provides an internal audience for this private encounter, the Vistula itself ("La Nymphe de cette Onde écoutant leurs discours"), which delivers a message to the royal characters: "Elle semble leur dire, encore que sans voix / Que ses Campagnes, ny ses Bois / Ne peuvent souffrir le Tartare" (vv. 231-33). The Queen is then presented as sharing the opinion of this animated river ("LOUYSE, à qui le cœur augure / Quelque sinistre évenement, / Est dans le mesme sentiment," vv. 226-28). The subject of the conversation, as it appears in direct discourse between Louise and Casimir, is thus presented first by animation of the landscape, to which the poem's human characters, as if echoing, give voice.

Both in this conversation (strophes 27-31) and in the later Vision of the Queen, the events leading up to and following the battle of Warsaw are presented by Louise, Casimir, and their deceased infant son. This second dialogue is introduced, like the first, with reminders of its imaginary and indirect quality. Louise, after a night of sleep, "voit, ou croit voir, à regards suspendus, / Un Enfant . . ." (vv. 707-08); the Vision, furthermore, is only transmitting a message from above and is not the immediate source of what he says ("Le tres-haut, qui me fait parler, / M'en a commandé la descente," vv. 732-33). The two speakers have a temporal specialization. Louise recounts the treasons that led up to the war and that motivated Casimir's calling on the Tartars for help, while the Vision speaks of the future, including the result of the decision to employ "enemies" of the faith and God's final judgment. The Queen, Casimir, and their son are all in turn speakers and listeners, as is the Nymph, so that the poet is not the immediate speaker, nor the reader the immediate listener of these internal messages.

Several visual descriptions use an indirect or internal viewer. These range from the minor, but not insignificant, "Et qui voit sa retraite admire en sa conduite, / Une mobile fermeté" (vv. 107-08), that posits an impersonal viewer distinct from the speaker, to the use of the actors of the poem as viewpoints. Their view intersects temporally the poet's view of the past beauty of the Polish court:

> Aprés ces preuves mutuelles
> De leur pure et forte amitié,
> Ils vont revoir, non sans pitié
> Des choses tristes et cruelles.
> Ils vont revoir ces Parcs, ces Lieux jadis si beaux

Où tous les celestes Flambeaux
Sembloyent sousrire à la Nature,
Et de qui maintenant, ô sanglante avanture!
Les Rossignols sont des Corbeaux.
(vv. 181-89, strophe 21; cf. strophe 9)

The past image of the gardens, assumed by the poet for his own experience in the opening section of the poem, is here expressed as the perception of the characters of the poem. The events on the battlefield are also viewed by the Queen as internal spectator. She watches the progress of the Polish troops through a telescope from the ramparts (strophe 60).

This is an aspect of the poet's description *in absentia* of the events in Warsaw that could be called visual overcompensation. That is, the attention to detailed visual evidence seems particularly acute, as if the poet, as witness, were basing his assertions on a quasi-empirical induction from external display. These "observations" are still more interesting because of the final undependability of the external signs. For instance, describing the Queen's activities in general:

Ce n'est pas qu'un regret sensible
Ne fasse en elle ses efforts;
Mais s'il la surmonte au dehors,
Au dedans elle est invincible.
Dans le coup imprévu d'un si rude malheur,
Sa raison souffre sa douleur.
Sa constance approuve ses larmes;
Et jamais à soy-mesme elle ne rend les armes
Qu'elle ne montre sa valeur.
(vv. 118-26, strophe 14)

Saint-Amant also describes the flush that rises from the Queen's breast (strophe 33). Her reactions to the battle as she watches from the ramparts are both a very indirect vision of the vicissitudes of the battle ("Si-tost que l'un ou l'autre plie, / Elle en reçoit l'impression," vv. 532-34) and a "reading" of the Queen's emotions in her visible gesture:

Le geste du dehors peint celuy du dedans;
Selon les divers accidens
Elle s'agite, elle s'altere;
Conservant toutesfois de son beau caractere
Les signes toûjours evidents.
(vv. 527-31)

Louise, as she leaves the cannon that she has aimed across the river towards the Swedes, is covered with a queenly perspiration ("Une sueur illustre et belle / Se roule en torrents precieux / Sur son visage gracieux, / Qui des appas est le modelle," vv. 613-16). In isolation, these descriptive details might seem simply the kind of extreme variations in magnitude of focus to which the readings of De Mourgues have sensitized us in the works of Saint-Amant and Théophile. On the one hand, there is a battle raging between thousands of soldiers and, on the other, there is the precious and charming perspiration of the Queen, her blush, and her gestures. But in the context of the poet's frequent reminders that he has not seen any of the events described, we are conscious that *a fortiori* he is not witness to these minute details. They are therefore purely emblematic and literary—they are verisimilar and they proceed from inside to outside, they are *signs* of what the Queen is (or should be) feeling. The poet's use of these signs to tell us what is happening is a simulation of witnessing a present event, a simulation that, by its extreme precision, succeeds in decoding part of the larger military event from the minute signs of the emotions of one of the peripheral observers. Or, to be more exact, the poet encodes the larger event in a smaller event, thus creating a series of levels of meaning by interposing between speaker and event, and hence between reader and event, a number of layers of perception. The split in the focus of the poem, by giving more attention to these minute manifestations of queenly emotion and self-control than to the direct description of the battle itself, privileges perception over action and prepares for the final meditation on the value of military glory.

Meanwhile, the actions of the king are not absent from Saint-Amant's account, but the poet, by a kind of inverse preterition, takes back, with the anonymous murmur of an internal speaker, the praise that he gives in his own voice. When speaking directly of the actions of Casimir, Saint-Amant tells of his valor: "Et du grand CAZIMIR le renom veritable / Par-tout en sera mieux semé" (vv. 593-94); but when the rout of the Polish troops is described, the poet reports what the soldiers see and say: "Chacun regarde autour de soy / La terre de membres jonchée, / Et chacun en secret, l'ame d'horreur touchée, / En murmure contre son Roy" (vv. 555-58). The poet is therefore not murmuring about Casimir; he is simply reporting (fictitious) complaints by nameless characters.

After this indirect presentation of the events of the battle, the Vision of the Queen not only provides a convenient way of inserting into the idyll matters that are not within the temporal limits seen by Saint-Amant as proper to the genre, nor simply another mediating device that distances the event still more from the speaker-poet.[8] It provides the key to seeing the relationship between event and message, appearance and meaning, that the opening section of the poem had announced. The insistence on the internal resolution and virtue of the Queen and its manifestations or concealment at different moments has prepared us for a movement away from appearance towards a more abstract and inward truth. At the end of the Vision, attention is transferred from the content of the dialogue between Louise and her transfigured son—the question of the causes and outcome of the reliance on Tartar (non-Christian) aid—to the existence of the message itself. Louise passes from being an observer and sometime participant in the military events to being the recorder of her dream in writing: "Elle songe en allant à ce qu'elle a songé; / Elle s'en fait un abregé / Pour y songer toute sa vie; / Elle en est tout ensemble et confuse et ravie, / Et son mal en est soulagé" (vv. 923-27; I underline). The poem here reaches an even higher level of indirect representation than when the future events were described by the actor-vision. Louise now represents to herself the appearance and sound of the messenger as he delivered his message:

> De ce divin Objet tout luy charme les sens;
> Ses yeux doux, ses traits innocens
> Forment en elle un beau miracle;
> Ils vivent dans son cœur, et de sa voix d'Oracle
> Elle y peint jusques aux accens.
> (vv. 932-36, strophe 104)

The prophecy of the Polish defeat has become a memory (or a mémoire, in Louise's summary of it) of a prophet prophesying. After the disappearance of the Vision, the poet's object and the principal character depart entirely from the battle. Louise goes to enter a convent, "Vivre à soy-mesme, et servir Dieu" (v. 921). It is at least curious that, when telling of the Vision and the departure of the Queen, the poet no longer qualifies his statement with reminders of the uncertainty of his information. Is this because the events themselves are sufficiently extraordinary as to require no reminders of this sort? This is probably an approximation of the answer, but it can be restated as being a movement from one type of discursive "event" (the historical— public, epic, in principle destined to be stated and restated in many discourses and therefore relative, in the sense that it must withstand confrontation and comparison) to another (the lyrical —one which is internal, unverifiable and not subject to the confrontation of several discourses on the same event). In the closing strophes, the poem is no longer "about" the battle of Warsaw, but about messages, meaning, and memory. A divine and secret message about the battle is summarized in writing and will serve as the basis of future meditations.

A circle is closed by the return to the theme and rhetoric of the opening section. The Queen, who as actor in the battle and reflector of it can be considered a mediating figure between the hero and the poet, gradually moves towards the purely reflective and linguistic as she makes a summary of her dream and withdraws into the relative solitude of monastic life. The Queen then disappears as character in the poem in the 110th strophe. The poem thereafter mentions her only in general terms, rather than in connection with specific acts:

> J'admire de sa Vie et le lustre et l'Odeur;
> J'admire la sainte froideur
> Qui de l'Eloge la détache;
> Mais, j'admire sur tout, que lors qu'elle se cache
> C'est lors qu'on voit mieux sa splendeur.
> (vv. 995-99)

The Queen's "disappearance" constitutes, with the visual disruption of the stream in the sixth and seventh strophes, a signal of transition between event and anagogy; at the end of the poem this takes the form of a return to the level of moral generalities with which the poem begins. The Queen leaves the poem in two ways. First, as character, for the "event" on which the poem is based is now over and she has ended her public life by her retreat. And second, as possible reader or beneficiary of the poem, for her retreat is interpreted by the poet as an indication of her rejection of the basis of heroic poetry, its value as laudatory memorial. Paradoxically this rejection of praise—"la sainte froideur / Qui de l'Eloge la détache"—is the final proof of her splendor—"lors qu'elle se cache / C'est lors qu'on voit mieux sa splendeur." This concept and similar expressions appear in the opening strophe of the poem: "Accordons l'ombre de la splendeur" (v. 9). The fact that the *shadow* of the beginning of the poem refers to the poet's retreat only reinforces the rhetorical coherence of the text, its passage from the meditative retreat of the poet to the meditative retreat of the principle character, a passage which underlines one aspect of the problem of this *genre*, the heroic idyll with a religious basis: how does one reconcile the splendor of the hero with the silence of the religious eclipse to the world? Saint-Amant's answer seems to be in the treatment to which the "event" of the poem is subjected. Even if we leave aside the explicitly didactic opening and closing sections in which the event is shown to be only an accident in man's passage towards spiritual permanence, the displacement and qualification of the story of the battle between Casimir and Charles of Sweden show that this epic event *in itself* is not of major importance to the poem. The poet's frequent assertions of his incapacity to provide direct and veracious testimony of the battle, his precise, or overprecise visualizations of the encounter and appearance of the troops, his heavily conventional invocations to his Muse during the story of the battle, his assertion that the reports from the battlefield are only "bruits passagers"—all of these ways of treating the heroic event reveal a devaluation of military action in favor of reflection on the significance and possibility of literary treatment of such objects. The fact that the poet can at the same time indicate his uncertainty about the *facts* of the battle and write about the battle with the extreme detail of the actions of the princes is a reminder that Saint-Amant is not writing about *this* battle, but about the entry of the concept of "battle" into literature. The sixty-fifth strophe, for instance, is a rewriting of innumerable encounters between the great epic figures who seek each other in the crowd of faceless and nameless soldiers:

> L'autre, enflé de sa confiance,
> Dont il se fait tout son appuy,
> D'en venir aux mains avec luy
> A presqu'autant d'impatience.
> Ils sont et l'un et l'autre, et forts et hazardeux;
> Ils escartent dejà tout d'eux
> Pour montrer leur mortelle adresse;
> Il se joignent dejà, mais une horrible Presse
> Tout-à-coup se jette entre-deux.
>
> (vv. 575-85)

Saint-Amant did not have to see any reports of this sought encounter to know that it was part of the literary model of princely combat. Normally, the reader would have no reason to call such a detail into question. Few readers of Saint-Amant's period or of ours would seek in the heroic text a pure transparency, and if anything is seen "through the text" it would be another epic text of which the current one assumes the tradition. But the effect of Saint-Amant's questioning of the basis of his writing in its contrast with the reports that contemporary readers might have seen (or might not have seen, or would have forgotten—and the poet takes it upon himself to remind them of the distinction between historical and literary) makes the detailed representation of the battle take on a resonance of pure literarity.

The importance of these distinctions becomes apparent in the next to the last strophe, where Louise's detachment from praise is contrasted with the infidel's dependence on it: "Arrière, cette fausse gloire / Dont se prévaloit le Payen; / Toute sa vertu n'estoit rien / Qu'un vain desir de la Memoire" (vv. 1000-03). The Pagan not only values glory after it is atttained, but acts solely to gain a place in a certain poetic discourse. His actions are therefore directed towards words—"le seul but de l'Estime / Le disposoit à l'action" (vv. 1007-08). The Pagans in question are not the Tartars of earlier in the poem, as the tense indicates, but the Greco-Romans, on whose cult of memory the epic tradition is founded. This is a manifestation of Saint-Amant's resolute modernism. He has chosen to deal with a similar type of heroic action and assume some of the traditions of the "epic" genre, but he is writing a new genre, of which La Généreuse is the second realization and the more explicitly critical.[9] This is a heroic poem that attacks the cult of Memory.

At the end of the poem we can see the full effect of the opening section, the scene of the poet. That scene contains the anagogic level of the poem, the meta-discursive function of the work
as a whole, and the outlines of the visualization of the heroic
scene. The trees of the opening scene represent the moral gran-
deur of the heroine, who exemplifies the timeless virtue of resistance to adversity through spiritual strength:

> Il est bien vray, monstrant leur force,
> Qu'agitez, et non abbatus,
> Ils ont besoin d'autres vertus
> Que celles qui n'ont que l'écorce.
> Il faut que de leur cœur, un esprit vigoureux,
> En des assauts si dangereux
> Parte et monte de branche en branche;
> Et que pour s'affermir, si-tost que l'une panche,
> L'autre se releve sur eux.
> (strophe 5, vv. 37-45)

This is one of the opening strophes that deals with the anagogy
that will underlie the heroic scene that follows. But its lesson of
the dominance of the spiritual over the contingent and temporal
contains a meta-discursive message as well. We are here given the
key to a number of problems of reading that will appear in the
account of the two days in Warsaw. There is, first of all, the particular insistence on the dichotomy interior/exterior that we find
later in the descriptions of Louise, whose gestures, involuntary
and voluntary, sometimes mask and sometimes reveal the more
important inner state. When the Queen disappears from the world
by taking refuge in a convent, this anagogy of the hidden spiritual
strength becomes more explicit. The effacement of the external
splendor of the Queen permits us to see her internal splendor.
The generality of this figurative use of the trees is then exemplified in the person of the Queen, an historical figure whose life
itself becomes symbolic.

The immediately preceding strophe of the opening section provides a meta-discursive lesson of even greater scope. It addresses
the question of the distinction between truth and error that is
part of the problem of the difference between the reports of the
battle and the poem in which Saint-Amant treats the event. The
apparent utility of both truth and error is the basis on which the

poet will erect the text that follows. Looking at the reflections of the trees in the water, the speaker says:

> Mais, comme en la seule apparence
> Leur sommet est precipité,
> L'erreur mesme, et la verité
> M'instruisent de leur difference.
> Ils sont toûjours debout, ils souffrent cent debats,
> Ils s'obstinent dans les combats
> Des plus effroyables tempestes;
> Ils portent jusqu'au Ciel les honneurs de leurs faistes,
> Et rien ne les peut mettre-à-bas.
>
> (strophe 4, vv. 28-36)

Here the poet is writing the same lesson that we will encode in the battle sequence.[10] The apparent reversal of the trees in the reflecting surface of the water is the representation of the disgraces and misfortunes of the world (cf. "les arbrisseaux / Me semblent renversez dans l'Onde; / Et pour peindre à mes yeux les disgraces du monde, / De leurs bras ils font leurs pinceaux," vv. 24-27). But since this reversal only affects the appearance, it signifies that the disgrace that it figures is only apparent, not real. This commentary is important, not so much for its moral lesson, which is a commonplace, but for its designation of the way in which it can be read. The error in the landscape of the opening section is useful error, an illusion that serves as vehicle for a lesson on a level of value that goes far beyond the level in which the illusion is actually an "error." Furthermore, in order for the viewer of this scene to extract (or, in fact, to impart) meaning, he must be aware that there is a difference between the appearance—the overturned trees in the water—and the reality of the upright position of the trees. The poet is alerting us to the difference between the use of appearance for what can be written into it and read out of it and the mere fascination with appearance as a value in itself. It is hardly surprising later on to find that the poet first casts doubt on his own representation of the battle in Warsaw and later on the whole project of memorializing such events. If we went no further than the epic element of the poem, we would be at the level of what is called in this section *l'écorce*.

The visual aspects of the scene of the poet are related in still another way to the following heroic scene in Warsaw. The poet's comments on the imaginary character of the descriptions of what happens on the Vistula (strophes 18, 36) have their beginning in his comments on how the opening scene is related, in the poet's act of enunciation, to the other scene. The spatial arrangement of the opening scene is to be superimposed on the events told later, while the climate of the opening scene is metaphorically related to the emotional character of the warfare in Poland:

> Tout ayde à mon dessein, tout en cette Saison
> Si muable en sa liaison,
> Sert à m'en ebaucher l'Idée:
> Elle est rude, elle est belle, et mesme est secondée
> Par l'assiette de la Maison.
>
> (vv. 14-18)

The *assiette* or situation of the manor house on its estate suggests the situation of the palace with its garden near the Vistula. It makes little difference where the poet was, in biographical terms, when he wrote *La Généreuse*; what matters is that the poet in this way makes the two scenes interdependent on the levels of spatial description, anagogic meaning, and meta-discourse.[11] He also shows the growth of the epic scene out of the scene of the poet in such a way that the poet's idea is primary. The later development of the Idea in the events in Warsaw is comparable to the useful error of the reflected trees.

By the end of the text we are thoroughly sensitized to the problems set forth in the opening scene, and the poet returns to them still again, though without the support of the visualization of the scene of the poet. The last four strophes relate still more closely the comments on the composition of poetry and the moral lesson. The Pagan is shown as creating a life based on appearance, on the hope of having his deeds written, while the Queen is shown as living only for inner reality, the reality earlier described as being under the bark of the trees, and as separating herself from Praise. The world of appearance and of human praise that the poet claims for the epic here yields to the splendor of disappearance, "lors qu'elle se cache / C'est lors qu'on voit mieux sa splendeur." The last strophe is an attempt to put into words the splendor of the invisible by mounting the ladder of spiritual refinement in the ineffable:

Dieu ne veut l'Homme que pour l'ame,
L'ame, que pour la volonté,
Il faut que sa seule Bonté
L'esmeuve, la touche, et l'enflame.
Enfin, il ne demande, à qui respire au jour,
La volonté, que pour l'amour
L'amour, que pour l'honneur suprême,
Que tout Ange luy rend, qui n'est dû qu'à Luy-mesme,
Et qui couronne un si beau tour.

(vv. 1018-26)

The poem thus concludes with a series of effacements. First, the battle gives way to the divine messenger, then the Queen disappears into the convent and separates herself from the language of the heroic poem itself, then the world disappears into the substance of God and the angelic praise.

The presentation of any event must utilize the "grid" of tenses available to the writer or speaker, for language demands some assumption of temporal viewpoint. No sentence can be realized in the potentiality of the infinitive. The choice of the present tense as the general basis for *La Généreuse* significantly runs counter to the traditional choice of the preterite for the statement of historical or legendary event. The use of the present to convey both the scene of the poet as he composes his poem (and the related interventions of the author throughout the text to accentuate his act of composition and his absence from the heroic scene) and the events in Warsaw would in some ways seem to offer a chance for the effect of an "eye-witness" account, strengthening the authority of what is told. But the poet's insistence on his uncertainty and absence instead reduces the vividness of the present to the moment of the poet's composition. The identity of verbal tense joined with the emphasized distance deflates any potential of *im*-mediacy by making us think more about mediation. The absence of the preterite further serves to weaken any claim of historical objectivity, a claim that is attached by convention to this tense. But the perfect and the future do dominate in one section of the text, the strophes on the Queen's Vision. The Queen tells the infant messenger the past events that led Casimir to ask for help from the non-Christian Tartars, and the infant tells in the future tense the consequences of this offense to God on the part of Casimir. Why does Saint-Amant enfold in his text a section in which this strong temporal dimension stands out against the flattening present tense of all the rest? In no sense could this be attributed to any "necessity" imposed by the "nature of things," for, from an extra-textual standpoint, all the events recounted in the battle and in the infant's prophecy (except for the reception of Louise into heaven after her death) were equally past by the time Saint-Amant wrote and published his poem. Instead Saint-Amant chose freely here, as in other texts, this kind of interruption of temporal continuity.

The effect of these tenses in this indirect enunciation is evident. The Queen's use of the perfect (*passé composé*) makes her assume a highly personalized view of events that led to the battle of Warsaw. Of the rebellious vice-chancellor Radziejowski, she says, "Il nous a suscité l'Occident et le Nort; / Il a couru de Port en Port / Pour nous livrer à la tempeste" (vv. 797-99). It is from within the section of the Vision that the reader has the first historical explanation of events that in any way cause the conflict. Her words take on more authority from the nature of the person speaking; she is offering a view of history as part of the royal couple that commands events on earth. But because of this authority, which is also a responsibility, she is engaged in a special kind of discourse here, *pleading*. Her words are a reaction to the predictions of the infant in the future tense, a future tense that has the highest degree of certitude of all statements in the poem, for it comes ultimately from God and not from a fallible human speaker. The temporal dimension of the poem is strongest, then, in the passage which ostensibly escapes the outwardly historical, since the Vision is an invisible event. This suggests that the important temporality, in line with the thematic of the rest of the text, is that of man's personally assumed responsibility for past events and the judgment of God in the future.

Some of the same problems of heroic poetry that appear in a religious idiom in *La Généreuse* are stated eighteen years earlier in *Le Passage de Gibraltar* (published in 1640) in a "burlesque" idiom. In *Le Passage de Gibraltar*, as in *La Généreuse*, the poet and the hero are presented as acting in space. But while the poet in *La Généreuse* occupies his own poetic retreat outside of the space of the event, in *Le Passage de Gibraltar* the poet presents himself as an actor in the naval expedition which is directed by the poem's hero, the Comte d'Harcourt. Spatially, the poem is much simpler than La Généreuse, and the "plot" of the poem in the primary scene of the poem, that in which the speaker is present, could hardly be simpler; the French fleet moves through the straits of Gibraltar from the Atlantic to the Mediterranean without incident. The poem moves chronologically from early to late, while the fleet moves from west to east. If this activity seems barren of narrative interest, it is because the poem is based on a non-event. The dramatic tension that exists from the beginning of the poem in the expectation of an encounter with the Spanish fleet is completely released in the last strophe when the poet announces that there will be no encounter and that the day will be consecrated to la débauche.[12]

The secondary scene (strophes 36-54) consists of a prophecy of Spanish defeats in later naval battles in the Mediterranean, battles in which the French fleet under Harcourt took possession of Sardinia and the Iles de Lérins. This internal story is linked in many ways to the passage of Gibraltar—it is about the same actors, the fleet under Harcourt; it is chronologically and spatially the outcome of the movement westward begun in the primary scene—but it is distinct from the limits imposed by the poet on the frame-narrative of the passage of the straits during a single day.

The poem is organized, then, in two contrasting sections: an outer one beginning and ending the poem, in which the poet presents himself as temporally and spatially within the story, and an internal section, in which the poet more briefly reappears, both as actor and speaker. In some ways this organization parallels La Généreuse, where there were three principal scenes—poet's woods, the distant scene in Warsaw, and the Queen's prophetic Vision. In Le Passage this organization is less complex, simplified into the scene of the poet and his own prophetic vision. In both texts, however, the poet has created a distance between himself and the historical events.

Looking more closely at the organization of the primary scene of Le Passage, we see that the poet's matter, in the absence of an event to narrate, is a very special kind of description. The term "description" is approximate, for the poet is doing something more akin to a playful kind of allegorical *reading* of the ships of the fleet. Each ship has a name and an insignia, and the poet considers these names not as proper nouns, but as common nouns, thus freeing them from their immediate reference so that they can function in a fictive and figurative level linked to the scene of the poet at one point and thereafter parallel to it. The names or insignia are developed, in most cases, into small stories.

These allegorical readings are uninterrupted from strophe 20 to strophe 34, where they yield to the prophecy, but they begin as early as strophe 10:

> Le Portrait du fameux Chapeau
> Devant qui le Turban supréme
> Tremble, et n'est en sa peur extréme
> Qu'un Beguin, cresté d'oripeau;
> Ornant, d'une auguste maniere,
> Cette martiale Baniere,
> Nous arme mieux qu'un Morion
> Pour briser la teste derniere
> Du rogue et nouveau Gerion.
>
> (vv. 82-90)

If allegory can be described as the use of a pre-existent series (in this case a paradigm) to support and articulate another series, then this strophe is a concise allegory. The insignia of *La Cardinale*, a relatively inglorious *patache* (small coast-guard vessel) being the cardinal's hat, the series that Saint-Amant has at his disposal to figure the conflict between France and its enemies is "head-gear." The feared turban is reduced to a nunnish or infantile *béguin*, etc. Saint-Amant proceeds similarly with the bird names of ships (strophe 20, the *Coq* makes the Spanish Lion tremble; strophe 21, the *Cygne* comes to sing the swan song of the Spanish fleet), land animals—unicorn, lion, ermine, hare, and others (strophes 25-29), abstraction (Fortune and Hope, strophes 30-31), and the saints (strophes 32-34). The late medieval taste for allegory and allegorism is here combined by Saint-Amant with his own predilection for texts in which the speaker serves as a passive viewpoint or center around which unfold the descriptions or literary insertions of *La Solitude* or *Le Contemplateur*.

Most of these allegorical segments are temporally independent of the framework of the poem—they belong to a permanent literary mythos expressed in the present tense—but occasionally they point towards the destination of the fleet and the awaited battle (e.g., of the *Hermine*, "Et si le poil s'en contamine / Ce ne sera qu'avec du sang," strophe 27). They have a thematic relationship to the battle, since they all reflect some kind of menace towards Spain, but they are removed by their figurative and mythic quality from the scene of the poet as character.

The prophetic section, distanced from the speaker in its futurity, also makes use of this allegorical reading, thus creating a further effect of stasis or intemporality. After evoking the cries of anguish of (the island of) Sainte Marguerite in the Iles de Lérins, Saint-Amant continues:

> Son cher amy saint Honorat
> Triste et confus, en fait de mesme,
> Et sa jouë en ce dueil extréme
> Change en pâleur son nacarat;
> Il souspire, il pleure la perte
> De sa haute Couronne verte
> Que le noir Autan reveroit,
> Et que l'œil du bleu Melicerte
> Depuis cent Lustres admiroit.
> (strophe 46, vv. 406-14)

Saint Honorat is the second of the two Iles de Lérins, and his green crown was the woods that had covered the island before the Spanish cut them down. The verbs of the allegories of the prophetic section are in the present and the imperfect, not in the future. This reduces the potential dynamic of "movement towards" that could be strongly invoked with the future and creates segments that are deprived of all continuity in historical progression. They are not claimed for the past, yet they are not strongly assigned to the future. They are "descriptive" of recognizable geographical locations, but these places have been transformed into *personae* which can only be conceived in a literary topography that is permanently unfinished and non-punctual, the time of the enduring imperfect of the eye of Melicertes of mythology.

Not all of the prophecy, to be sure, is written in this way. The major part of it is in the future tense, and within this future the poet appears as both singer and actor. In the midst of the battle he says,

Là, le Rebec je quitteray
Pour mettre la main à la Serpe;
Là, laissant pour Bellonne Euterpe
Les plus Mauvais je frotteray;
Puis aprez, comme un Sire Orfée,
Ayant la cervelle eschauffée
Du fumet si doux à Bacchus,
Je celebreray le trofée
Basty des armes des Vaincus.
(strophe 53, vv. 469-77)

The poet has here projected himself, *en abîme*, into the prophetic future while representing himself as doing what was planned, and at this point in the poem still expected, for the day in which the frame-story occurs. The poet thus presents himself, in the present, but in the future of the battles of the Mediterranean—something that he is in fact doing in the present, but in the future *tense*. The verbal tense and the posture of prophesying have become means to create an internal distance between the poet and his actions, both as fighter and as singer, exploiting the semantics of the future tense. If a speaker makes a statement about himself in the perfect (*passé composé*), the action attributed is distanced from the moment of speaking but assumed into the definition of the speaker. The distance between the speaker and an action set in the future tense is not parallel to one in the past, for, at the most, it reveals an intention, a fear or other possibility. Therefore, Saint-Amant, by using such a tense, both represents himself in a certain activity and disavows any claim for the historical reality or realization of the activity. This disavowal is strengthened, in the case of the act of singing (or the content of the song), by the figurative creation of still another veil between the speaker and his object with the drink, the "fumet si doux à Bacchus," a veil that is already present in the primary scene, where the poet's first action is a toast.

If we move back from this examination of the text to the level of reception that includes the poet's presentation of the poem in his preface, we can see the special quality of the future here. Saint-Amant has used it to fictionalize himself. He has chosen the future tense to tell actions that were already past at the time the poem was composed. The prophecy shows surprising accuracy because it is not prophecy, but history written in the future.

Saint-Amant's arguments for the use of this prophecy, as he states them in the preface, are not altogether convincing. He claims, essentially, to have been bound by historical accident to write his poem this way, as a "burlesque" (or "bourlesque"), with the prophecy to take the place of what did not take place: "Au surplus, si nous eussions combatu en ce Destroit, comme nous ne fismes point . . . j'eusse employé d'autres couleurs en la composition de ce l ableau que je ne fis; il n'y auroit rien paru que d'heroïque & de serieux . . . Mais ne s'estant versé que du Vin en cette Journée, au lieu du sang que nous nous attendions de respandre, je le continuay du mesme air que je l'avois commencé, & inseray dedans par maniere de Prophetie, selon les bons tours du Mestier, le Combat donné quelque temps apres."[13] The literary genre, burlesque epic or "Caprice héroï-comique," is dictated, in this description, by historical occurrence. Certain things, in this case a "non-event" as I have called it, can only be written about in a certain kind of language. So far, this seems to be a classical argument based on decorum. But why was Saint-Amant bound by the occurrences of this particular day when he had at his disposal the truly heroic events that figure in the prophecy? The answer to this problem is Saint-Amant's claim to have begun the poem on the day of the passage of the straits: "ces Vers que je commençay la mesme Nuict dans l'Admiral . . . je m'y laissay aller brusquement, à l'aspect des Estoiles qui nous regardoient boire & fis, le Verra, & non la plume à la main, les premiers couplets de cette Pièce."[14] But the two arguments do not fit together. Either Saint-Amant was bound to the day's actions by his desire to keep the verses he had composed (and in this case the poem would have had to be mock heroic, regardless of the historical occurrences, since the tone of the first verses already contradicts the "rien . . . que l'heroïque & de serieux"); or he felt free to alter his project according to historical contingency, and in this case he could have assumed a different temporal standpoint and written a heroic poem beginning with the actual engagement of fighting with the Spanish.

Rather than explain the real reasons for the burlesque tone and the use of a prophecy, Saint-Amant's preface serves primarily to underline the poet's consciousness of temporal viewpoint, of what we have called the scene of the poet, and of the "tricks of the trade," as he calls the insertion of the prophecy. Saint-Amant chooses to underline within the work itself both his own compositional activity and his distance from the heroic event. He de-activates the event by placing himself to speak at a moment when nothing happened and then filling, as he indicates, the void thus created with two kinds of secondary story: first, the animation of the objects and insignia that surround him in the scene of the poet and, second, the prophecy in which heroic event is removed from statement of "reality"—i.e., the quality of the primary statements of the speaker, within which the scene around him takes on the substantiality of the speaker himself.

Numerous other works of Saint-Amant in the 1640s show variations on this distancing of the speaker from the events of which he speaks. The *Epistre héroï-comique* (1644) to Gaston d'Orléans on the conquest of Gravelines contains a prophecy (retrospective once more, since the events prophesied had already taken place at the time of publication of the poem); the letter form, by which the poet pretends to be distanced from the hero at the moment the event is taking place; an animated indirect speaker in the form of the statue of Henri IV on the Pont Neuf by which Gaston, his son, is addressed; and within the prophecy the representation of various other types and levels of language that signify Gaston's victory: the blind man singing of Gaston on the Pont Neuf, speeches of the burghers who welcome Monsieur with "mille belles harangues," the *Te Deum*, the fireworks representing luminous dragons in the sky, the toasts which make the name "Gaston" resound from all sides. The effect of this multiplication of languages is an increase in the praise addressed to Gaston, since the poet claims simply to transmit the praise he hears around him. But it also constitutes distancing of the poet from the utterance of praise of specific action of the hero, a layering and indirection that we have seen elsewhere.

In the "au lecteur" of *Les Nobles Triolets*, Saint-Amant points out one of the principal characteristics of the enunciation of this text about the siege of Paris during the Fronde of 1648-49. There is an utter indeterminacy of speaker; the poet refuses to accept responsibility for his utterance: "tantost c'est moy qui parle:

tantost c'est le tiers & le quart: tantost c'est le Bourgeois qui dit de bons mots à sa mode: tantost il y a quelque suitte: et tantost il n'y en a point du tout. Que si, contre mon dessein, il s'y estoit glissé quelque heresie d'Estat, je la desavouë."[15] All of the speakers speak in the first person, and without this warning we would assume a continuity of *persona*. With his "tantost c'est moy qui parle" Saint-Amant is dividing the "je" of the poem into a series of *separate* fictions as one way of attaining his primary goal of separating himself, as extra-textual entity, from the dangerous elements in his text. He could simply have written, "c'est un autre qui parle . . . ," but he has found a way of creating an even greater protection by warning the reader not to assume *any* continuity of speaker. This is an attitude, in addition, that fits excellently the strophic form chosen. The rhyme scheme of the triolet (a b a a a b a b / c d c c c d c d) gives each triolet a great distinction from its neighbors, and the repetition of the two opening verses at the end of the triolet gives a strong sense of closure.

When Gérard Genette writes of *Moÿse sauvé* (1653) that it manifests, by its multiplication of levels of enunciation, "l'intérêt du poète pour l'acte représentatif lui-même,"[16] he is stating a characteristic of all of Saint-Amant's later work. The second heroic idyll goes still further in its presentation of the problems of representation, testifying to a growing self-consciousness or irony in Saint-Amant's view of his poetry. The result of this progression is a transference of interest from the historical reality of the event itself to the process of representation.

One could say that Saint-Amant has managed to make of narration a description. Genette has said of the distinction between the categories narration and description that it is without "semiological existence" and consists only of "differences of content."[17] In other words, the distinction is not one of means (*signifiant*) but of meaning (*signifié*). By this token one would expect Saint-Amant's heroic and mock-heroic poetry, on the grounds of its content (event or even "anti-event"), to be frankly narrative. But such devices as the Vision of Louise, the references to the changes in her outward appearance (manifestation of emotion) as she watches the progress or difficulty of the Polish troops, the assumption of the significance of the event into the anagogic level in the beginning and end of *La Généreuse* all fracture the narrative into a series of static moments that seem more inherently "descriptive." The breaking up of the story leads up to the paradox of Zeno's arrow; the event is the combination of apparently static moments. The poet's playful use of dramatic tension in *Le Passage de Gibraltar*, the adjournment of the "event," and the use of the allegorical development of ships' names and insignia produces a similar "de-narration" of what would, in terms of content alone, seem intuitively to be descriptive.[18] Could we not turn Genette's affirmation around and conclude that the only difference between narrative and description is semiological? The great innocent world of things is without distinction until distinction is made by the observer, and content is not content until it is contained in a form which determines that content. A battle may be described, if seized in a single moment, or narrated, if seized in successive moments. Thus the distinction between narration and description is purely a matter of the aspect under which a thing is perceived and conveyed. The distinction that appears in the *Passage de Gibraltar* and *La Généreuse* between the version of the historical occurrence given and the other, more orthodox version that is glimpsed and rejected is purely semiological and evidence of the author's awareness of what he could do to history and with history by means of language.

I have so far been neglecting the modern distinction between discourse and history (*histoire*) as elaborated by Emile Benveniste (or the difference between "commenting" and "telling" in Harald Weinrich's terms). The reason for this neglect, and for avoiding as much as possible the term "history" for the telling or recounting of event in these texts, is that there is relatively little "history" (in the modern sense) in Saint-Amant's later poems. The objective character of historical narrative, the dominance of the third person, and the absence of allusion to the speaker and to the circumstances of enunciation—none of these theoretical characteristics of Benveniste's *histoire* are apparent in Saint-

Amant's poetry of heroic event. It is true that Saint-Amant obtains a kind of impersonality, but he does so not by avoiding the first person but by increasing its frequency, creating a pluri-personality in which there are many voices telling the story.

In some ways it seems as if the structural basis of the early solitude poems and the early poems of classical legend (*L'Arion*, *L'Andromède*) has been fused and injected into the project of heroic poetry. *La Solitude*, for instance, is a series of designations of places through which the speaker passes. His only action is to sing. Is this not similar to the "action" or inactivity of the hero of *Moÿse sauvé*, who simply floats down river and whom Genette so aptly describes as "plutôt vagissant qu'agissant"?[19] Or to the poet in the *Passage de Gibraltar*, whose actions consist, in the primary level of the text, of pointing and saluting in toast?

More then the introduction of an event or a "story" to the texts, what distinguishes the later heroic poems from *La Solitude* is a multiplication of the centers of enunciation and of action.[20] In *La Généreuse*, the poet is composing while the Queen is enduring the Swedish assault; in *Le Passage de Gibraltar*, the poet is watching while Harcourt leads the fleet. But the categories are not so distinct as they seem at first; Saint-Amant habitually breaks down the barriers between poet and hero by attributing to both similar enunciatory roles. In *La Généreuse*, as we have seen, the Queen becomes not only the source of an important historical discourse within the text, but she also writes out the summary of the Vision (just as the poet does for us). And the Queen retreats into a meditation that resembles, by its separation from the world of events and its pondering of eternal truths, the poet's meditation. In *Le Passage de Gibraltar*, the poet never represents himself as engaged in combat, nor does Harcourt become historian. But the two are united in one common linguistic activity—and indeed it seems to be the only activity in the primary level of the story—toasting, and hence, naming: "Pour me pléger il prend sa couppe / Où petille et rit le Nectar, / Et s'escriant Masse à la trouppe, / Sa voix estonne Gibraltar" (vv. 159-62). In *L'Epistre héroï-comique* the poet's admonition and celebration is not undertaken by Gaston, of course, but it is shared with many other voices.[21]

This consideration of the patterns of enunciation in Saint-Amant's later poems of heroic event contains several important lessons to guide us in future readings. First of all, it shows that the occasional claims to poetic inspiration resulting in careless and carefree texts of little internal coherence—the frequent pose of Saint-Amant with glass in one hand—is a fiction belied by the persistence of complex structures in texts of various lengths and from different periods. It shows, furthermore, that the devices used to tell the story of Moses are not isolated but are part of a long-standing interest in the problems of heroic poetry. Most of all, it should put us on guard against the claim, made by Sayce, among others, that Saint-Amant "was a poet for whom the essence of poetry was visual evocation."[22] Visual evocation and "literary pictorialism" are means by which Saint-Amant relates—but at a distance—the speaker to the content of his speech. Therefore, they enter into the general category of indirect presentation that so frequently characterizes Saint-Amant's poetic discourse.

Chapter IV

THE RHETORIC OF PROCESS IN HISTORICAL CONTEXT

In a brief analysis of several major texts by Saint-Amant, I have suggested a reading that is centered upon the creation of a fictive representation of the relationship between the author and the reader. Fictive, because the poet's representation of this relationship is *performed* within the text itself much more than it is referred to in the world beyond the poem. In each of the works we have studied, and in the groups of poems that they exemplify, this relationship is built upon a recognition of the roles of the benefactor and of the poet. In each we have seen an explicit designation of the poetic function. In *Le Contemplateur*, the speaker is a figure that performs a specific series of verbal acts according to the general forms of meditational usage while incorporating the addressee into the performance by depicting him both as model and as "collocutor." At the same time, the meditational form is undermined by reminders of the speaker's adherence to a secular rhetoric of praise. In such poems as *Le Cantal*, among the "feasts," the speaker is assuming a role in a social exchange which produces a reversed imitation of the extra-textual situation of poet and benefactor. In *La Généreuse*, the speaker's separation from the actions attributed to the aristocratic benefactor/ heroine moves the interest of the poem towards the problem of the text. By a series of internal mirroring devices the heroic characters become themselves performers of the kind of linguistic-symbolic activity that is in fact the realm of the poet, so that the heroic event becomes more profoundly indicative of the activity of a poet than the poem serves to transmit a representation of that heroism. The problem that recurs then in these texts is the problem of the role of the poet, a role that is repeatedly considered in reference to a social, economic, and historical realm common to poet and designated audience.

Edwin Duval has demonstrated in a masterful way in his *Poesis and Poetic Tradition in Early Works of Saint-Amant* that Saint-Amant establishes his own role by a reworking of passages from his predecessors, particularly of Ovid and Ronsard.[1] Duval's work will go far towards correcting the misconceptions about the spontaneity and literary naïveté of Saint-Amant's work. The description of his approach to Ronsard's *Franciade* epitomizes this relationship of mocking the earlier work "by inverting its sources of inspiration, parodying its diction in such a way as to give a new and appropriate meaning to the tired nautical metaphor piously copied by Ronsard, choosing as its epic hero a lyric poet of precisely the Ronsardian kind but one whom the Pléiade had almost entirely overlooked, and finally by fusing a recognizable lyric and epic elements of the classical tradition into a coherent whole."[2] It would be difficult to go beyond the brillant detection and restoration of Saint-Amant's textual foundations accomplished in Duval's readings of *La Solitude* and *L'Arion*.

Nonetheless, it is important to point out that Saint-Amant's preoccupation with the representation of poetic activity and his creation of a *persona* are not limited to the stance taken towards the earlier writers. The poems studied here all have in common both implicit and explicit inscription of the poem's relationship to a world of discursive convention and social exchange. The poem demonstrates the way in which it arises from an interweaving of these different discourses. One of these is, as Duval has shown, the poetic tradition represented by Ovid and the Pléiade. But Saint-Amant also includes in his networks of allusions the contemplative discourse, table conversation, court flattery, Pont-Neuf gossip, printed journalism, toasts, and other conventional linguistic forms. Saint-Amant's work abounds in manifestations of the form-in-a-form, of situations in which the *personae* of the poetic fictions are shown in the act of discursive exchange, and in which the frontiers of each type of discourse serve as reminders of the existence of language as object and product.

The present study has consisted of close readings of texts with attention to the poem's manifestation of the *means* among which the speaker (and beyond him, the implied author) chooses the form or forms from which he will make his own performance.

At the risk of a breathtaking and breathless expansion of the horizon of this study, I think that it would be appropriate to conclude with some suggestions and even some speculation on the historical context in which Saint-Amant elaborated this rhetoric and on the way in which this rhetoric makes of the poet a great transitional figure in literary history.

The seventeenth century saw a redefinition of the role of the poet. This redefinition was not, in general, a favorable one; or at least it did not tend to increase the dignity of the lyric and epic poet in the hierarchy of literary practice. What does Saint-Amant's poetry tell us about his conception of the changes that were occurring in his art? Such matters as the function of metaphor and the choice of words, topics of much debate in Saint-Amant's day, are closely related to the rhetoric of process that we have found in his texts.

Saint-Amant's place in the general transformation of seventeenth-century poetics has been obscured by two errors of literary history. The first is the myth propagated by the poet himself that he was only a carefree versifier, a "joyeux compagnon." The second is the fragmentary notion frequently maintained about the factions that were struggling over a language and its use. We frequently classify the opponents of Malherbian doctrine according to their prosody, not according to their conception of language and poetry. Yet the struggle is really not about the specifics of verse form but about what importance should be assigned to figurative language and to lexical meaning. The two misconceptions taken together reinforce one another. If we take at face value the mythology of Saint-Amant as *personnage*, it becomes harder to conceive of his participating in a serious conflict over the principles of literature. It becomes still harder, therefore, to imagine an ideological grouping in which Saint-Amant, the "libertine" poet, finds himself on certain issues side-by-side with Jansenists and with Montaigne's literary executor, Marie de Gournay. Yet, in the opposition between the tenants of a literature of signification and a literature of signifiers, between a literature rich in conceptual invention and a literature based on the disposition of surface elements and the restriction in rhetorical elements (i.e., the prohibition of "obscure" metaphors and mythic allusion), Saint-Amant finds himself closer to the Renaissance aesthetic than to Malherbe's.

An anecdote about Malherbe held that he had seven chairs in his room and that he locked his door when they were all taken. Should anyone come to visit after that, Malherbe would shout that he must wait until someone left. The anecdote continues that Malherbe had only seven metaphors as well and that ideas could wait . . .[3]

The principal battleground of these two groups—we could call them the Old Poets and the New Poets—was the "quarrel of Metaphor." The New position is generally anti-metaphorical. Metaphor can be tolerated to the extent that it is imperceptible, lexicalized, or, as we say today, "dead." One classical popularizer said of language, "Le beau langage ressemble à une eau pure & nette qui n'a point de goust; qui coule de source; qui va où sa pente naturelle la porte."[4] Or, as Charpentier wrote, "Il faut prendre garde dans l'usage de la Métaphore, de ne se jamais servir que de choses très-connuées."[5] The extravagant figures of Saint-Amant are far from the ideal of a language without taste, clear and imperceptible. On the contrary, Saint-Amant draws attention to the complexity of his language and to the poetic act. At no point in his work can one forget that someone *made* this text, that it is a *text* and not a pure natural spring, that it is part of a social exchange that presupposes and underlines *difference* and not sameness. Is there theoretical reflexion on figurative language in the century that can help us understand what is at stake in the use or refusal of metaphor?

Cartesian and Jansenist rationalism moved from inside to outside as from the most certain to the least certain, not from the evidence of the senses to the conclusions of the world's spectator. Rousset has suggestively observed that the scorn of certain Jansenists for metaphor is probably a result of the discontinuity they felt between the mind and the world, a result of the original Fall that had closed the way to any firm knowledge not impaired by a supernatural and miraculous faith. Of Nicole, Rousset writes, "il a si bien perdu tout sens de l'univers comme unité organique qu'il leur cherche et leur trouve quelque origine impure."[6]

Although Nicole was to find a new basis for figurative language, it is certain that the discontinuity between man and nature, felt by theistic rationalists as well as by agnostics, plays a role in the use of physical objects and their qualities both as figures in the narrow sense (tropes of comparison and metaphor) and in the wider sense (all pattern in discourse, particularly description).

The discontinuity between man and nature is related to the possibility and desirability of mimesis. The Aristotelian doctrine of imitation was a commonplace of seventeenth-century literary theory. It became one of the touchstones of *le naturel* set forth as an ideal by numerous critics and theoreticians during the seventeenth century. Yet, one of the problems with this concept, as the art historian Giulio Argan has pointed out,[7] was that few agreed on what was to be imitated. Carried to its extreme, the idea of imitation resulted in formulations that seem to abolish the work of art itself and certainly eliminate any sense of an aesthetic structure or mediation. Bouhours, later in the century, seconds Valincour's censure of the passage in which Madame de Lafayette represents Sancerre's laments in *La Princesse de Clèves* because the character's words are incompatible with his supposed affliction. Sancerre as character seems too "ingenious" to be truly grieved. Similarly, of a passage in Tasso, Bouhours observes that "Les jeux d'esprit . . . ne s'accordent pas bien avec les larmes, & il n'est pas question de pointes quand on est saisi de douleur."[8] It would be easy to show that this observation derives from a voluntary confusion between the categories of the true and the verisimilar or between nature and conventional representation. But the significant concept in these comments, for our purposes, is the suppression of the consciousness of poetic mediation. If this process is followed to its extreme, there is no consciousness of the difference between imitation and object imitated, hence none of the admiration which is supposed to derive from the comparison between the two.

This difficulty did not escape another neo-Aristotelian, Carel de Sainte-Garde, who started from the same commonplace ("il n'y a rien qui plaise tant aux yeux qu'une chose bien imitée") but arrived at an apparently opposite prescription for poetic practice. Returning to the extreme example of a disagreeable object to imitate, the one that has served from Aristotle's *Poetics* to the modern *arts poétiques* of Baudelaire's *Une Charogne* and Williams Carlos Williams' "To a dog injured in the street," Carel points out that a cadaver "tout plombé & groüillant de vers" would be insufferable if real ("véritable") but agreeable if well represented: "La cause de cela est que l'homme naturellement aime à connoistre & à raisonner."[9] The theorist's attention has moved here from the imitation to the process of reception and judgment. This is one of the most important shifts in emphasis of any of the neo-classicist theories, for it parries all objections to pleasure in *mimesis* by setting forth clearly the orientation towards *process*. The objects themselves, the representing object and the represented one, do not have a value in themselves and separately, but only in relation to one another, or rather, only in virtue of the *act* that permits that relationship (the act of *poesis*) and of the act which perceives the relationship and infers the antecedent act (in an act of reading). The practical corollary of this description of mimesis is the necessity of awakening the readers' and viewers' attention to the contrast between the two objects. Carel calls this provoking the reader's "syllogistic force": "Nous avons dit . . . que la Poësie delectoit par une multitude d'objects dont elle remplissoit l'imagination, & par des traits hardis qui révelloit le raisonnement & qui obligeoient les Lecteurs à comparer les efforts de l'art avec la conduite de la Nature, Et notez que par la Nature, j'entens icy méme tous les autres Arts excepté la Poësie. En un mot tout ce qui est au dehors d'elle . . . il faut que l'imitation represente toûjours son sujet d'une maniere surprenante & qui oblige toûjours les spectateurs à syllogiser."[10] For a comparison to take place, a distinction or separation must be present, and this emphasis on the distance between the two objects and on the latent tension to be resolved by the reader's "syllogism" is the opposite of an aesthetic of transparency that characterized much French literature of the period.

Carel de Sainte-Garde's formulation of the doctrine of mimesis emphasizes the distance between the representing and the represented and in so doing calls attention to the mediation and therefore to the texture of the work of art. The *traits hardis* are *hardis* because they are not noticeable, because they cannot be taken for granted or "looked through" without the exercise of a certain reasoning. These *traits* are, furthermore, internal to the level of meaning in the work; they are what would be called *ornements* or *conceptions* in the language of seventeenth-century poetics and belong to what is widely called today the form of content (as opposed to the substance of content and to the level of expression). The mediation to which the reader's attention is awakened is not that of sound (rhyme, metrics, stanzaic form) but that of the various semantic components of the text. Carel gives several examples of the ways in which the poet can provoke the reader's syllogistic force. One of them is the re-forming of the apparently natural order of "events": "Ces récits [in "l'ordre naturel" or chronological order] donnent quelque sorte de plaisir, mais un plaisir languissant. L'imagination en est trop morne. Le Poëte heroique en cherche une plus éveillée & qui exerce avec plus d'activité cette force syllogistique ou comparative qu'a notre esprit."[11] Here again we see Carel's insistence on what the representative act adds to the habitual order of perception (as codified into a "natural" order) which in itself is too dull for the work of art. Starting with the commonplace of imitation as creation of likeness, the theorist has evolved a doctrine of *imitation as the production of difference*, of the creation of a better and more immediately perceptible order.

One source of the comparative act is the confrontation, made by the reader, between the order of narration to which he is accustomed and the non-chronological or episodic order of the successful heroic poem. Another source of comparative appreciation is the insertion of a second level of representation within the text. For this Carel describes one of the most ancient of poetic devices, but one that was particularly characteristic of the currents that were later described as mannerist and baroque: "Il n'est pas jusqu'à la Peinture, bien que d'ailleurs elle luy soit tres-semblable, qui ne doive être mise au rang des choses naturelles, au sens que je le prens en cette rencontre. Car un Poëte qui décrira les portraits figurez dans une tapisserie, doit obliger ceux, à qui il parle, de syllogiser, & de comparer les traits de sa plume avec les traits de l'aiguille ou du pinceau."[12] An internal distance is created within the text so that reading becomes the detection and evaluation of relationships between different levels or methods of representation. The visibility of the speaker's gesture, so to speak, is increased by this multiplication of representational relationships (in this example there are the persons portrayed, the tapestry, the language in which the tapestry is described) and by this provocation of the reader into a conscious decoding of these relationships.

This clear and forceful refusal of a mimetic transparency in the work of art finds allies in the rhetorical doctrines of Port-Royal. Although the Jansenists are sometimes said to have opposed figurative language, particularly metaphor, the Port-Royal logic of Nicole and Arnauld justified figurative language by giving a new and powerful explanation for its effect.

Nicole argued that "toutes ces figures qui s'écartent de la manière ordinaire de parler ne se font pas souhaiter par elles-mêmes. Elle ne sont . . . que des remèdes au dégoût de la nature."[13] As Jean Rousset observes, Nicole's argument is based on the supposition that man is fallen and that figurative language is an indication of "cette faiblesse de la nature qui se rebute de la vérité toute simple et toute nue."[14] But this is only one step in Port-Royal's consideration of figurative language. In La Logique (1662) of Arnauld and Nicole, figures are shown not to point to the world or the referent but towards the production and reception of the message. They note,

C'est encore par là qu'on peut reconnoître la difference du stile simple & du stile figuré, & pourquoi les mêmes pensées nous paroissent beaucoup plus vives quand elles sont exprimées par une figure, que si elles étoient renfermées dans des expressions toutes simples. Car cela vient de ce que *les expressions figurées signifient outre la chose principale, le mouvement & la passion de celui qui parle*, & impriment ainsi l'une & l'autre idée dans l'esprit, au-lieu que l'expression simple ne marque que la vérité toute nue.[15]

The importance of this statement can be seen best in light of the semantic theory of the *Logique*, where words are described as the vehicle first for their proper or denotative meaning ("signification précise") and secondly for connotative meanings ("idées accessoires"). These connotative meanings are divided into two groups: (a) those that convey the disposition of the speaker ("l'image d'une disposition") and (b) other attributes or other facets of the object denoted (a category also described as "idées ajoutées").[16] What is important in the description of figurative language in the *Logique* is the emphasis on the first group of connotative meanings. Rather than leading us from one idea to another within the sphere of the object, figurative language is one means of drawing our attention to the sphere of relations between subject and object and to the prescription of an attitude towards the object and even towards the message itself.

Arnauld and Nicole illustrate this conception with a phrase from Virgil and its transformation:

Par exemple, si ce demi vers de Virgile: *Usque adeone mori miserum est!* étoit exprimé simplement & sans figure de cette sorte: *Non est usque adeo mori miserum:* il est sans doute qu'il auroit beaucoup moins de force. Et la raison en est, que la premiere expression signifie beaucoup plus que la seconde. Car elle n'exprime pas seulement cette pensée, que la mort n'est pas un si grand mal que l'on croit; mais elle représente de plus l'idée d'un homme qui se roidit contre la mort, & qui l'envisage sans effroi: image beaucoup plus vive que n'est la pensée même à laquelle elle est jointe.[17]

We find here the same distinction as in Carel de Sainte-Garde between the "dullness" of the ordinary or objective message and the "liveliness" added by devices of conception—that is, verbal strategies for calling attention to the act of the speaking subject —or rather, to the act of the thinking subject. It is not the surface of the message—the euphony, the conventions of syntactic order, the enunciation—that is underlined, but rather the moment in which a conceiving subject arranged the content in a certain way. This displacement of interest from object to subject and from the meanings which cluster in the *ordre naturel* to those which are imposed on the discourse by the speaker is quite possibly related to the late Renaissance and Cartesian discovery of the primacy of the subject. Messages "about" objects become interesting to Descartes and to the Jansenists as emanations of a thinking subject. The Jansenists' emphasis on this secondary message telling us how the speaker felt about the object and how we should feel about it (e.g., in our reading of the Fathers we learn how we should dispose ourselves towards the truths of religion) is, of course, different in its aim from the aestheticism of Carel de Sainte-Garde, but the desire to create in the reader a consciousness of the scission between object and the significant form through which we glimpse that object is an example of the sense of subjective mediation with which texts of some circles are penetrated in the seventeenth century.

Without wanting to suggest a political or religious link between Saint-Amant and Jansenism, I think that there are certain common elements in their conception of rhetoric. The justification of figure and of vocabulary is, in both the *Logique* and in Saint-Amant, not in terms of generic decorum nor in connection with the matter ("la vérité toute nue") but in reference to the provocation in the reader's consciousness of the sense of discourse as production. In both cases the poetic activity is defined primarily on the basis of the implicit contact between two subjectivities, the reader's and the author's. Thus, in spite of the general reputation of Port-Royal as polemically engaged in the struggle against figure, what we have seen in these passages is significant for its non-ornamental quality. Figure may be added to "la vérité toute nue," but it is *not* added to the poetic process itself. Instead, figurative construction *is* the poetic process, the poetic process making itself visible as a transaction. Similarly, in Saint-Amant, it would be difficult indeed to consider the figurative aspect of his texts as ornamental, and, in the texts we have examined, the choice and organization of the figure seems linked tightly to the author/reader exchange.

This sense of activity of writers in the shaping of conception appears in the seventeenth century not only in the theory of literature but also in a great historical transformation that was imposing itself or being imposed—the massive transformation in the French lexicon. This change, frequently linked with the names of Vaugelas and Malherbe, can be situated symbolically, if not causally, in March 1638. It was in that month that the Académie decided not to compose the dictionary of old words that it had planned a month earlier to undertake.[18] But this decision is the ratification of a change that had begun long before and involved modifications in both linguistic theory and in the economic and political situation.

The humanistic doctrines of the great sixteenth-century poetic movements, especially the Pléiade, were devoted to the study of the classical tongues, attentive to the progress of the classical revival in Italy, and eager to enrich the French language with borrowings and neologisms. This linguistic and especially lexical project was not born of a fascination with language in itself, but of the need to enlarge the vernacular to accommodate new poetic forms and inventions, to say things in French that had not been said before. The doctrine of imitation is inseparable from the project of expansion of the semantic capacity of the French language. For the poets of the Pléiade the fine divisions in the semantic substance of French were one of its chief virtues. Henri Estienne in his *Précellence du langage françois* praises the wealth of technical terms and the richness of the vocabulary of the crafts.[19] However, the poetic lexicon did not always demonstrate a corresponding richness, and Peletier felt that the poet should accept a program of vigorous linguistic expansion and inclusion in order to permit a proportionate enrichment of invention (or imagination) in poetry. Peletier expresses a problem in poetic semantics that reveals the seriousness with which the lexicon was considered: "Car sans point de doute, la chose la plus déplaisante aux hommes érudits est de se voir abondants en inventions et défectueux en parler."[20]

The sixteenth-century emphasis on expanding the language was based on the primacy of invention in writing and evaluating poetry. When the New Language of the seventeenth century was formed, its values were the opposite. The change affected the form of content, the meaning, permitted in French and not simply the surface characteristics. Many of the words dismissed by the code of good usage were necessary words, even in the eyes of linguistic reformers themselves. Vaugelas remarked, "J'ay une certaine tendresse pour tous ces beaux mots que je vois ainsi mourir, oppriméz par la tyrannie de l'Usage, qui ne nous en donne point d'autres en leur place, qui ayent la mesme signification et la mesme force."[21] But Vaugelas did not combat usage and instead codified the New Language, furnishing arms to this "tyranny." Malherbe's pruning of old words, technical expressions, lower-class words, and foreign words is related to his distaste for figurative language and his denigration of poetic invention: "Il avoit aversion contre les fictions poétiques," wrote Racan of his master.[22] Both lexical and rhetorical attitudes assign greater value to the phonetic and metric substances of the text at the expense of its semantic substance. The early opponents of the New Language had seen the consequences of these changes. Mlle de Gournay, in her denunciations of the "Poëtes jettez au moule de ce temps . . . valets de la rhyme et de la Grammaire, legeres aydes & simples suivantes de la Poesie," argues the necessity of signification and design.[23] She claims that the older poets chose their expression with the aim of expressing an invention or idea.[24] The Poet is the one who can say what others cannot, who can find ways to convey a meaning that others feel but for which they lack the forms of expression:

la conception et l'enonciation fortes et puissantes, ne vont non plus l'une sans l'autre, que les deux roües opposites d'un chariot. Mais qu'est-ce que discourir fortement? c'est dire ce qu'on doit et veut dire, et ce que les autres veulent, et ne peuvent point, ce qu'ils cherchent, et ne trouvent point.[25]

The fashion of creating severe metric and lexical limitations was criticized by Chapelain in a letter to Mlle de Gournay in which he agrees with her that invention on the conceptual level is the foundation of poetry. As a consequence, he recognized that Malherbe was ignorant of poetry: "Je vous dis qu'il tournoit mieux les vers ni que moy ni que vous mesme. Mais je vous dis aussi qu'il ignoroit la poësie, de la sorte que tous les maistres des bons âges l'ont connu." In the same letter Chapelain even notes that poetry is independent of verse and can exist without the metrical forms.[26]

By treating metaphor as if it were a simple element of vocabulary and by banishing, as Mlle de Gournay says, all metaphors "hors celles qui courent les rües"[27] and therefore making a poetry "une Prose rymée, et la plus mince & superficielle de toutes les Proses,"[28] the new poets were on the way towards a theoretical abolition of meaning as a criterion for poetry, since relatively limited figures, *topoi*, and words would recur with growing frequency. Gournay's objection is echoed by Arnauld's distinction between poetry and prose, a definition which runs counter to the fashion of formal perfection:

la Poësie, qui s'est toûjours distinguée de la Prose, en ce que son langage doit être plus orné, plus vif, & plus figuré. Cela est vray sur tout de la Poësie hebraïque, parce que ce n'étoit peut-être qu'en cela qu'elle étoit distinguée de la Prose, n'y ayant gueres d'apparence qu'elle consistast en un certain nombre de pieds ou de syllabes, les unes breves, les autres longues, comme la poesie grecque & latine.[29]

Thus, for Arnauld, as for Gournay and Chapelain, the essential nature of poetry is its conceptual structure and the prosodic elements are "accidental" or, in modern terms, secondary.

All those who write about poetry during the first half of the seventeenth century are acutely aware of the struggle over the degree of prosodic and lexical restriction. Some complain, as we have seen, about the reduction of emphasis on the conceptual level, while others see the challenge of Malherbe's concentration on formal surface. Much more important than the specific metric and rhyme forms adopted by Malherbe is his valorization of limitation itself. "Sa grande innovation," writes Fromilhague of Malherbe, "n'est pas seulement d'avoir transformé en impératifs telles règles de la poétique, c'est aussi et surtout d'avoir, dans la création, accordé à la règle une valeur en soi. . . . Pour Malherbe . . . les obstacles sont eux-mêmes créateurs."[30] This "renversement des valeurs" that Fromilhague has shown in the work of Malherbe should open our reading of seventeenth-century texts to a much broader outlook. We can now hazard the hypothesis that even the return to old forms such as *rondeau* and *villanelle*, a revival usually seen as a revolt against Malherbe, is a continuation of the emphasis on prosodic constraint. Even if the *précieux* poets do not always practice the particularly majestic forms favored by Malherbe, they continue the practice of ingenious manipulation of highly restricted linguistic material.[31]

The polemic between defenders of a conceptual tropic poetic and the proponents of a poetic of linguistic surface is part of a larger economic and political transformation. It is not accidental that the baroque phase of Malherbe's work, *Les Larmes de Saint Pierre* (1587), belongs to his life as a provincial member of the *noblesse de robe*, in a particularly noted humanistic center, Aix-en-Provence. His work was, at the time, outside the source of the New Language, based, according to Vaugelas, on the usage of "la plus saine partie de la Cour."[32] The great writers of the sixteenth century had been of the provinces and had frequently accentuated their regional ties. They had emphasized the humanistic revival with its Greek and Latin, its study of mythology, its consciousness of the desire to enrich French with words from the world of the learned. They had, as Peletier noted, a pride in the ability of the poet to integrate into his language words from all spheres, including the arts, the crafts, and agriculture. They had frequently been magistrates and active in the particularly fervent humanism that thrived in the provincial *parlements*. To list their social characteristics is to enumerate the *bêtes noires* of the language of the court. Words belonging to the provinces, to the *bourgeois* of any city, to artisans, to lawyers, and to scholars (pedants) were excluded from "le bel usage."

As Gournay observed, the limitations of the New Language are the limitations of the courtiers' thoughts and expressions. Ideas must be omitted from the new poetry "si les choses qu'on exprime en Vers ou dans les discours Politiques & Philosophiques, sont hors d'usage des muguets de Cour, reconneus tres-ignorants pour la pluspart. . . . Comment exprimerions nous au langage de ceste espece d'hommes & de femmes, des choses qu'elle n'a jamais dites, ny conceües ny pensées?"[33] The passage of power from the *noblesse de robe* to the royal court is thus a basic cause of the rise of a language and poetry fundamentally different from that of the humanists—learned, conceptual, open-ended. The complaints and opinions of Mlle de Gournay are a clear and forceful indication of the interdependence of economic and literary change and prefigure the tragedy of her defeated class as it appears in the work of Racine.[34]

The movement towards the New Language, a conception which we have borrowed from Gournay and Vaugelas, must not prevent us from seeing a larger picture, a view available to us through the activity of Saint-Amant himself. For it is clear that Saint-Amant was neither entirely a defender of Renaissance humanism nor an advocate of a language or a poetry based on simple effacement of the preceding century. Instead we can see that the "New Language" itself and Malherbian poetics are no more indicative of the actual modernity of the seventeenth century than is the work of Saint-Amant. For it is only by the practice of a critical and inventive use of the past that enduring change can come about. Such a use of the past is represented by a literary mode, championed by Saint-Amant, known in academic circles of the time as the grotesque and to Saint-Amant himself as the *bourlesque*. The close relationship between vocabulary and mode appears in Saint-Amant's volunteering for the task of collecting burlesque terms for the *Dictionnaire de l'Académie* in December 1637.[35] It is evident from Saint-Amant's poetry that archaic, popular, and technical vocabulary abounds in burlesque or grotesque verse. Words that had once been used in heroic works or theoretical works on the epic find themselves demoted to the status of archaisms, fit only to appear in works that openly accept their separation from the dominant historical movement of the court.

Historians of the burlesque from Brunot to Bar[36] have shown at length the large proportion of archaic expressions in burlesque poetry, but they have not underlined sufficiently the effect of this historic change on the form of the texts produced under the influence of a transformation that is apparently temporal but can only be grasped within a single, hence momentary or synchronic, work. In other words, they have fulfilled the tasks of describing change and diachrony (Brunot) and the contours of a genre, or mode, within a single period (Bar), but without showing the discursive organization of texts that accept the duality of register imposed by the moment in which they were written.

Saint-Amant's texts are among those that manifest the consciousness of language, of the texture of the poem, that is constant in grotesque poetry. The grotesque is, indeed, a poetry of criticism, because at all times it calls attention to the means at its disposal, to the vocabulary in particular, and never becomes the transparent and euphonic pastime towards which Racan, for example, among the New Poets, was moving. The poetry of Saint-Amant shows the way in which the continuous development of a literary vernacular is split at a certain moment into the New and the Old. We find within a single period of the language two registers which coexist—they are perfectly synchronous—but are distinguished by the users of the language as diachronic. It would seem as if time had been used in a metaphoric sense to distinguish two simultaneous phenomena. In fact, the Old Language is not so much old as it is obsolete, *surannée*, struck by an exclusion from the vocabulary of a group that wished others out of existence. To say "Cela ne se dit plus" is to mean "Cela ne se dit plus *ici*," but in a way that exploits the privilege of time over space with the former's implicit irreversibility.

I began this study by claiming for Saint-Amant a certain complicity with Boileau's evocation of the poet of the cabaret, a complicity which in some sense seems to set a trap for the literary historian, willing to take the speaker's character for the poet himself. Do I mean by this that Saint-Amant is indeed an *attardé* belonging to a Lansonian backwater? Quite to the contrary, Saint-Amant appears as an author whose complex and ironic use of literary and linguistic history makes him one of the principal points in the lyric tradition, perhaps the principal *étape* on that road between the Pléiade and La Fontaine. It is to the non-Malherbians that fell the opportunity to maintain the historic consciousness and with it a critical stance before history, for denial of the past is not necessarily the best means to dominate it. The grotesque is not a mere byproduct of literary change, not a passive accumulation of what is cast off, nor is it a genre practiced by those who cling to the old ways and old words. It is rather the innovation which permits movement towards the kind of poetry that we find after Malherbe. For it is only by selective integration and by the movement of vocabulary from one register to another that literary change can fortify itself against reaction. Saint-Amant is neither Malherbe nor Marie de Gournay; he is instead the bridge that permits movement beyond their impasse.

The grotesque is, of course, only one aspect of Saint-Amant's work. One could not categorize *La Solitude, La Généreuse, L'Arion,* and so many others of his best texts as grotesque. Yet these works have in common with the grotesque works an insistence on the non-transparency of poetic language, on the processes of poetic invention and poetic reception. The historical difference between a poetry of semantic *invention* and what Saint-Amant seems to describe as a more fashionable poetics of *elocution* (or of prosodic structure) is directly addressed in the "Petarrade aux rondeaux" (1637). Apostrophizing "Double Homonime, et vous fine Equivoque," he writes,

> Aupres de vous les plus hautes pensées
> Sont aujourd'huy dans l'estime abbaissées;
> Les plus beaux sens, les termes les plus forts,
> Tous eshanchez rampent à demy-morts:
> Et le Caprice avecques sa peinture
> Qui fait bouquer et l'Art, et la Nature,
> Ce Fou divin, riche en inventions,
> Bizarre en mots, vif en descriptions,
> Ce rare Autheur des nobles balivernes,
> Quoy qu'inspiré du Demon des Tavernes,
> N'ose parestre, et n'a plus de credit
> Depuis qu'en Cour vostre honneur reverdit.
>
>   (II, 202)

Thus Saint-Amant launches a double attack against the court poetry that banishes terms—and with them meanings—and that transfers emphasis to the ingenious conquest of metrical obstacles, *la difficulté à vaincre*, at the expense of the divine madness of the imagination. Similarly, in introducing his heroic idyll, *Moÿse sauvé*, the poet explains that he does not want to observe the restrictions of the epic, preferring instead to have new rules for new inventions.[37]

Saint-Amant, the "libertine" poet, can be linked with the poetics of Jansenism and with those of the older humanist tendency represented by Marie de Gournay because of his emphasis on the poetry of conceptual invention and its semantic consequences. As Nicole argued, the basis of figurative language is the desire to convey the attitude of the speaker to the listener. It is part of late humanist insistence on the process of reading and writing, an insistence that runs clearly contrary to the transparency of the Malherbian poetic. Nicole invites the writer to guide the reader towards a critical appreciation of the poetic message by inscribing within the message the attitude that should be assumed at the moment of reading. While Nicole could not be associated with the specific content of Saint-Amant's poetry, the poetic he recommends is consonant with Saint-Amant's highly critical, self-conscious rhetoric.[38] Saint-Amant's fascination with older, now proscribed, terms and mythologies parallels Gournay's charge that the poetry of the court was deficient in its conceptual content. She commented that the New Poetry is based on crossing things out so that what is *left out* of a text makes it valuable.[39]

Saint-Amant certainly assumes an inclusionary stance comparable in many ways to that of Gournay, but his attitude towards his sixteenth-century predecessors differs markedly from hers. His is not a respectful conservatism but a frankly skeptical desire to make use of whatever he could find among the lyric and epic materials of the immediate past. Duval's intertextual study of *L'Arion* and the *Franciade* has shown in convincing detail the fruits of an approach which is neither that of Malherbe nor that of Gournay, but instead one that permits a much more explicit glorification of Saint-Amant's own poetic invention. In other words, Saint-Amant's relationship to the various non-Malherbians was twofold. On the one hand, Saint-Amant, like many others, was committed to a privileging of invention and thus of a rhetoric through which the reader would be provoked into a certain surprise at the successful conceptual artifice of the poet. On the other, in the matter of the lexicon and the literary canon, Saint-Amant was not defending but only using the works of an earlier period to produce a kind of dissonance that would serve his rhetoric of invention. Saint-Amant profits from his moment in literary history, just as Baudelaire does much later, by exploiting the tension between an exclusionary and an inclusionary aesthetic.

The attitude provoked by Saint-Amant's poetry will be, unlike that awakened by Malherbe, a constant awareness of the conceptual and generic categories involved and a negligence of the metric properties of his language. This poetic conception, written into the texts themselves, can perhaps be understood as a voice that listens to its song, that calls attention to the complexities of its fabrication and that actively involves the reader in the figurative elaboration of its message. Saint-Amant's poetry is a poetry of the listening voice.

NOTES

Preface

1. Odette de Mourgues, *Metaphysical, Baroque & Précieux Poetry* (Oxford: Clarendon Press, 1953), p. 99.
2. Ibid., p. 95.
3. Imbrie Buffum, *Studies in the Baroque from Montaigne to Rotrou* (New Haven: Yale Univ. Press, 1957), pp. 136-62.
4. Francis L. Lawrence, "Time and the Individual Consciousness in Saint-Amant's *La Solitude* and *Le Contemplateur,*" *French Review*, 46, Special Issue, No. 5 (Spring 1973), 36.
5. Ibid., p. 34. Lawrence even calculates the author's passage through "at least eight different psychological states in eleven stanzas," p. 38.
6. Yvor Winter's term, used by Wimsatt and Brooks in their *Literary Criticism: A Short History* (1957; rpt. Vintage Books, n.d.), p. 670.
7. Lawrence, p. 33.
8. Ibid., p. 37.
9. Françoise Gourier, *Etudes des Oeuvres poétiques de Saint-Amant* (Geneva: Droz, 1961), p. 178.
10. Jean Lagny, *Le Poète Saint-Amant* (Paris: Nizet, 1964), p. 64.
11. Christian Wentzlaff-Eggebert, *Forminteresse, Traditionsverbundenheit und Aktualisierungsbedürfnis als Merkmale des Dichters Saint-Amant* (Munich: Max Heubner, 1970), p. 81.
12. *Saint-Amant and the Theory of Ut Pictura Poesis* (London: MHRA, 1972), p. 23. In D.D. Cosper's unpublished dissertation, "The Literary Pictorialism of Saint-Amant," Univ. of Washington 1973, the problems of Rolfe's approach are largely overcome by a greater attention to the theoretical entailments of pictorialism. Cosper's approach does not fragment the text, but it does argue a reader response that, in my view, is rather too narrow; e.g., Saint-Amant "wants the reader to complete the description in a pictorial manner and to visualize what is presented as he would a painting" (p. 136).
13. Two recent studies of Saint-Amant, both of which came to my attention when the present study was largely complete, have reacted against the traditional reading. Robert T. Corum, Jr., *Other Worlds and Other Seas: Art and Vision in Saint-Amant's Nature Poetry* (Lexington, Ky.: French Forum, Publishers, 1979), deals with

Saint-Amant's poems as complex wholes. My work has intersected Corum's, primarily in regard to *Le Contemplateur.* Edwin Duval's *Poesis and Poetic Tradition in Early Works of Saint-Amant: Four Essays in Contextual Reading* (York, S.C.: French Literature Publications Company, 1980) reached me in typescript shortly before its publication. The patience and thoroughness of its tracing of the subtexts of several of Saint-Amant's major poems and the subtlety of its interpretations make of Duval's work an extraordinary contribution to our knowledge of this poet. Although my approach has been different, our findings strengthen the case for the view of Saint-Amant as self-conscious literary craftsman.

14. Aristotle, *The Rhetoric,* trans. Lane Cooper (New York: D. Appleton, 1932), p. 6 (1355b). I regret that Marc Fumaroli's *L'Age de l'éloquence: rhétorique et "res literaria" de la Renaissance au seuil de l'époque classique* (Geneva: Droz, 1980) did not reach me until after completion of my manuscript. Fumaroli's work considerably enriches the picture of rhetorical change that I have touched upon, particularly in my conclusion.

15. Wayne Booth, *Critical Understanding: The Powers and Limits of Pluralism* (Chicago: Univ. of Chicago Press, 1979), pp. 268-72.

16. For both designated audience and implied readers the "historically knowable" counterparts can be further distinguished from the flesh-and-blood people, whose lives will always, for the most part, be mysteries to us as they were to most of their contemporaries.

17. See Rosalie Colie, *The Resources of Kind: Genre-Theory in the Renaissance,* ed. Barbara K. Lewalski (Berkeley: Univ. of California Press, 1973), pp. 1-31.

18. "Aymant la liberté comme je fais, je veux mesme avoir mes coudées franches dans le langage," preface to the *Passage de Gibraltar, Oeuvres,* II, 157. I have used, except where otherwise noted, the edition of Saint-Amant's works prepared by Jean Lagny and Jacques Bailbé (Paris: Didier, Société des Textes Français Modernes, 1967-71) in four volumes.

19. Richard A. Mazzara, in his "Théophile de Viau, Saint-Amant, and the Spanish *soledad,*" *Kentucky Romance Quarterly,* 14 (1967), 393-404, shows that Saint-Amant's poem is somewhat more like a *soledad* than is Théophile's poem of the same title, but the resemblances Mazzara indicates are hardly convincing evidence of any influence of Góngora on the French poet or of a generic pattern, for they are simply "interest in nature," "disenchantment," and the presence of the sea.

20. Mieke Bal points out the persistent failure of criticism to define the "event," despite the frequent invocation of the concept in studies of narrative. See "Narration et focalisation," *Poétique,* 29 (February 1977), 107-27.

21. Cf. Samuel Borton's totally different use of the term in his *Six Modes of Sensibility in Saint-Amant* (The Hague: Mouton, 1966).

Chapter I

1. Louis L. Martz, *The Poetry of Meditation* (New Haven: Yale Univ. Press, 1954; revised 1962), and Terence C. Cave, *Devotional Poetry in France c. 1570-1613* (Cambridge: Cambridge Univ. Press, 1969). In addition to these general studies, there have been useful explorations of devotional methodology as influence on the lyric of individual poets, e.g., Lance K. Donaldson-Evans' *Poésie et méditation chez*

Jean de La Ceppède (Geneva: Droz, 1969), and Nancy B.W. Hafer's unpublished dissertation, "The Art of Metaphor in La Ceppède's *Théorèmes* of 1613," Univ. of Virginia 1976.

2. In his *Elegie a Rets, Oeuvres*, I, 27-32. I have attempted a general description of *La Solitude* in "The Rhetoric of Fragmentation," *Orbis Litterarum*, 33 (1978), 4-17.

3. The limitation to the life of Christ is typical of the "morning meditation," as described by Cave, pp. 48-57.

4. Cave notes that the analytic section is considered by many devotional writers to be the meditation proper. Cave, p. 30.

5. Cave, p. 27.

6. Cf. Hafer's description of "pseudo-composition," p. 110.

7. Cave, p. 305.

8. Ibid., p. 27.

9. The reader who has most clearly remarked on the relationship of the clues to the performance of a contemplation in this poem is Robert Corum. He has noted the mimetic tendency: "The religious orientation of many of the speaker's reactions conforms to the station and rank of his addressee" (*Other Worlds and Other Seas*, p. 33). But Corum, in keeping with his focus on nature poetry, does not permit himself to follow this insight into the rhetorical display. D.D. Cosper notes, though in a very different perspective, the contemplative aspect of this poem: "the meditative tradition had an influence on Saint-Amant which produced various results: A general and definitely pictorial one in 'Le Contemplateur'; a very subtle and humorous one in 'Le Melon' " (*The Literary Pictorialism of Saint-Amant*, p. 218). See also Cosper's "Saint-Amant: Pictorialism and the Devotional Style," *Romance Notes*, 17 (Spring 1977), 286-97.

10. In purely devotional poetry, further refinement in description is not only quite feasible but important. See Cave, p. 305. Hafer has demonstrated the usefulness of such analysis in her work on La Ceppède by relating types of metaphor to the structure of meditation.

11. Corum's analysis, with its emphasis on the "natural features of Belle-Ile" and on the speaker's reactions to these features differs from the reversal in precedence suggested here.

12. Gérard Genette, "L'or tombe sous le fer," *Figures I* (Paris: Seuil, 1966), pp. 29-38.

13. Lagny, *Oeuvres*, I, 56n.

14. On this concept, see V. Shklovsky, "L'Art comme procédé" (1917), trans. by T. Todorov in *Théorie de la littérature* (Paris: Seuil, 1965), pp. 76-97, and F. Jameson's comments in *The Prison-House of Language* (Princeton: Princeton Univ. Press, 1972), pp. 43-98.

15. Other examples of the re-making of the human form in other substances in this period are Ariel's song in the *Tempest* (I, ii) as well as Caliban himself, and the image of the Magdalen in Crashaw's *The Weeper*. The popularity of Ovid in the early seventeenth century is well established, and Saint-Amant owes to him the subjects of such poems as *L'Andromède* and *La Métamorphose de Lyrian et de Sylvie*. The Glaucus of *Metamorphoses*, book XIII, may very well be the basis of most of the poetic sea creatures. If the poet was thinking of this Glaucus, the *persona* of Saint-Amant's *Le Contemplateur* takes on another layer of meaning, as I suggest below.

16. For further evidence of the period's preoccupation with this frontier be-

tween beast and man from Montaigne to La Fontaine, see Erica Harth's "Exorcising the Beast: Attempts at Rationality in French Classicism," *PMLA*, 88 (1973), 19-24.

17. Jacques Bailbé and Jean Lagny are of this opinion. *Oeuvres complètes*, I, 64n. See also Cosper, p. 133 ff.

18. For the "picturesque" quality of the Last Judgment, see Buffum, pp. 156-61, Rolfe, and Cosper.

19. There is no space here for a general review of the pictorialist controversy. The best treatment is in Cosper's *The Literary Pictorialism of Saint-Amant* (1973), which contains a detailed and thoughtful analysis of *Le Contemplateur*. Many of the problems of pictorialism are resolved by Cosper's approach, but at the expense, I think, of an extension of pictorialism nearly to the point at which it absorbs the whole process of semiosis. Thus the very aspects that strike me as reducing visual effects in this poem are arguments in favor of pictorialism in Cosper's sense: Saint-Amant "obviously intends that their physical appearance and present activities betray their former misfortunes, but it is the poet who draws these conclusions and creates the drama" (p. 143). Thus the poem does not transmit the *visual* aspect of painting but the speaker's interpretation of information that *he* received as "visibilia."

20. Giulio Carlo Argan, *The Europe of the Capitals*, trans. from the Italian by Anthony Rhodes (Geneva: Skira, 1964), p. 49.

21. Cave has underlined affective adherence as a major aim of devotional rhetoric. Cave, p. 228.

22. Martz, *The Poetry of Meditation*, p. 27.

23. Cosper has noted the relationship between this evening reading and the meditative tradition, pp. 214-15.

24. Was the Passion too sacred to serve as the content of an explicit display of rhetorical gifts? Saint-Amant does not elsewhere shrink from parody of the eucharist (*Epistre, a Monsieur le Baron de Melay*, II, 230-53). However, in an address to a bishop he is apparently, once again, mindful of his designated audience.

25. Corum also believes that the conclusion undermines the impression of sincerity in regard to religious belief, but he does not detect any irony in Saint-Amant's affirmation of belief in Cospéan's power to confer worldly immortality on the speaker (p. 67).

Chapter II

1. Gourier, *Etude des Oeuvres poétiques de Saint-Amant*, pp. 85-98.

2. Boileau, *L'Art poétique*, I, 21-22.

3. Emile Benveniste, "L'Homme dans la langue," in *Problèmes de linguistique générale* (Paris: Gallimard, "Bibliothèque des Sciences Humaines," 1966), pp. 225-85.

4. Gourier emphasizes the "précision du détail descriptif" in these poems (p. 88).

5. Note, in this regard, Benveniste's argument that the "third person" is a "non-person" (pp. 255-56).

6. Jacques Pons, *Traité du melon*, rev. ed. (Lyons: Antoine Cellier fils, 1680), p. 33.

7. A.J. Greimas, *La Sémantique structurale* (Paris: Larousse, "Langue et Langage," 1966), p. 123.

8. Elie Vinet and Antoine Mizauld, *La Maison champestre* (Paris: Robert Foüet, 1607), p. 625. Melons have a large place in the gardening literature of the period, where particular attention is given to their tropical origin and the difficulty of growing them north of the Loire. The cantaloupe melon (*cucuminis melo reticulatus*) was the most recent of these migrants from warmer climates and brought with it the connotation of an Italian and papal origin (from Cantalupo, a country home of the popes); it came to France, some say, about 1495 on the return of Charles VIII from the Italian wars. Saint-Amant uses this connotation for a national contrast in his *Rome ridicule* (LXVIII): "Bref, je gite en melon de France, / Sur une couche de fumier" (cf. Claude Mollet's *Théâtre des plans et jardinage* [1652], where use of dung overcomes the melon's resistance to the Parisian climate). The melon's affinity for wine appears in Mollet's recommendation that the seeds steep in good wine before being planted (p. 153) and the taste of the melon could be improved by such contact. Pons claims (pp. 22-23) that by soaking the seeds in milk mixed with musk and amber one could obtain a melon of that aroma, precisely like Saint-Amant's (v. 2). Mizauld, Pons, and Du Perron (*Perroniana*) have much to say about its medical and sexual significance.

9. Martial Le Maistre accuses the fruit of *leze majesté* for its effect on Henry IV and describes a death by Melon: "Les infames effectz que produit céte plante, / Ourdissant les chaisnons d'une mort violante . . . / Voyla dans certains jours l'estomac panteler, / Des genoux chancelans les colomnes branler. / Une froide sueur decouler de la face, / Les membres s'engourdir d'une mortelle glace, / Un acre flux de sang racler les intestins" (p. 9). In Le Maistre's text Apollo is not the giver of the melon but the preserver against it, in his role as god of medicine (p. 5).

10. Saint-Amant himself mentions an example of the untouchability of that which is set aside for the gods. In *Rome ridicule* (1643), he alludes to the island in the Tiber formed by the wheat that the Romans had set apart for Mars and could not eat (strophe 44). For a thorough phenomenology of sacrifice and the "set aside," see Georges Bataille, *La Part maudite* (Paris: Minuit, 1967).

11. See Georges Mongrédien, *Etudes sur la vie et l'œuvre de N. Vauquelin, seigneur des Iveteaux* (Paris: Picard, 1921), p. 133. Des Yveteaux was blamed for this sacrilege.

12. The Chronicles of Pantagruel, "Roy des Dipsodes," conclude with the naming of their author, "feu M. Alcofribas abstracteur de quinte essence." The Fifth Book of Rabelais takes place in part in the "Royaume de la Quinte Essence, nommée Entelechie." Saint-Amant alludes to alchemy in *Le Cidre* and entitles one poem *La Naissance de Pantagruel*.

13. Cf. the similar encoding of mythic and linguistic qualities in the trees of the beginning of *La Solitude*.

14. *Oeuvres*, I, 277-78.

15. The Bernesque tradition, within which Saint-Amant's poem can be read, includes poems about foods similarly constructed with an alternance of suspense and revelation. See, for example, Antonfrancesco Grazzini's ("il Lasca's") poem, *Il Capitolo della Salsiccia*.

16. Cronos, son of Ouranos, is often identified with Chronos, Time.

17. For a general view of the burlesque, defined as a mixture of registers of language, in seventeenth-century France, see Francis Bar's *Le Genre burlesque en France au XVIIe siècle. Etude de style* (Paris: d'Artrey, 1960).

18. I regret not having seen Duval's treatment of *Le Melon* and *Le Fromage* in

Poesis and Poetic Tradition in Early Works of Saint-Amant before completing my study.

Chapter III

1. Thomas Greene, *The Descent from Heaven. A Study in Epic Continuity* (New Haven: Yale Univ. Press, 1963), p. 337.

2. Boileau, *L'Art Poétique*, I, 21-24.

3. Saint-Amant, *Oeuvres*, IV, 9.

4. What was new—and it would eventually have a profound influence on the writing of poetry (is it a coincidence that the epic virtually died in seventeenth-century France?)—was the creation of a new kind of text during the generation of Saint-Amant, the printed news medium. The *Gazette de France* of Théophraste Renaudot first appeared in 1631, and Saint-Amant's poetry is full of events that also were reported in Renaudot's pages.

5. Preface to *Le Passage de Gibraltar*, *Oeuvres*, II, 162.

6. For the conception of *histoire* as the impersonal third-person presentation of events—the distinction *discours/récit* as based on distribution of persons, pronouns (*je* vs. *il*, etc.) and of tenses (*passé composé* vs. *passé simple*, etc.)—see Emile Benveniste, "Les Relations de temps dans le verbe français," and "De la subjectivité dans le langage," in *Problèmes de linguistique générale* (Paris: Gallimard, "Bibliothèque des Sciences Humaines," 1966), pp. 237-50 and 258-66.

7. See Lagny's footnotes to *La Généreuse* (*Oeuvres*, IV, 4-62) and to *Les Pourveus bachiques* (*Oeuvres*, II, 213n).

8. Saint-Amant points out in the preface to *Moÿse sauvé* that he limits his first heroic idyll to half the time allowed the tragedy: "par une maniere toute nouvelle, je renferme mon sujet non seulement dans les vingt et quatre heures, comme le poeme dramatique est obligé de faire, mais presqu'en la moitié de ce temps-là" (*Oeuvres*, ed. Livet [Paris: P. Jannet, 1855], II, 143).

9. In the preface to *Moÿse sauvé*, Saint-Amant makes a general apology for literary modernism: "Sans m'arrester tout à fait aux regles des anciens, que je revere toutesfois et que je n'ignore pas, m'en faisant de nouvelles à moy-mesme, à cause de la nouveauté de l'invention, j'ay jugé que la seule raison me seroit une authorité assez puissante pour les soutenir; car, en effet, pourveu qu'une chose soit judicieuse, et qu'elle convienne aux personnes, aux lieux et aux temps, qu'importe qu'Aristote l'ait ou ne l'ait pas approuvée?" (*Oeuvres*, ed. Livet, II, 140). Thomas Greene also points out a major element of Saint-Amant's departure from epic traditions: "*Moÿse sauvé* is not only profoundly anti-heroic and anti-epic, it is also opposed to the voluntarism which its age brought both to art and philosophy" (*The Descent from Heaven*, p. 347). Greene also points out Saint-Amant's freedom from both classical and Christian tendencies (p. 340).

10. Jean Lagny finds that Saint-Amant "joue subtilement—trop subtilement—sur l'apparence et la réalité, présentes en même temps, selon qu'on regarde ici ou là" (*Oeuvres*, IV, 14n).

11. This is not to deny that if we had a certain knowledge of the location that Saint-Amant visualized to himself as he composed *La Généreuse* we could learn much about his compositional practices of selection and arrangement of detail. But even if

a real place is at the origin of this literary scene, the selectional process itself makes of the setting of the poem a fiction.

12. Admittedly, the tension that might build towards the non-discovery of the Spanish fleet is deflated from the beginning by the light burlesque language. This is another one of Saint-Amant's ways of distancing the reader from the "action" that purports to be the center of the poem.

13. *Oeuvres*, II, 163.

14. *Oeuvres*, II, 160-61.

15. *Oeuvres*, II, 225-26.

16. Genette, "D'un récit baroque," p. 210.

17. Genette, "Frontières du récit," *Figures*, II, 59-61.

18. I have pointed out that the miniature allegories of *Le Passage de Gibraltar* are "stories," but they are temporally disconnected from the "passage" itself.

19. "D'un récit baroque," p. 205.

20. This technique is already used in *L'Andromède* (1629) but in a much simpler tale. See "*L'Andromède*: The Myth of the Poet and the Hero," *L'Esprit Créateur*, 16 (1976), 116-24.

21. The *Moÿse sauvé* itself has several internal speakers, one of whom tells a story by describing pictures (Amram's story of Joseph).

22. "Saint-Amant and Poussin," *French Studies*, 1 (1947), 251.

Chapter IV

1. (York, S.C.: French Literature Publications Company, 1980).

2. Ibid., p. 134.

3. Racan, *Mémoires pour la vie de Malherbe*, in *Oeuvres complètes*, I, 273.

4. Bouhours, *Entretiens d'Ariste et d'Eugène* (Paris: S. Mabre-Cramoisy, 1671), p. 55.

5. Charpentier, *Carpenteriana* (Amsterdam: n.p., 1741), p. 217.

6. Jean Rousset, "La Querelle de la métaphore," in *L'Intérieur et l'extérieur* (Paris: Corti, 1968), p. 68.

7. Giulio Carlo Argan, *The Europe of the Capitals: 1600-1700*, trans. A. Rhodes (Geneva: Skira, 1964), p. 31.

8. Bouhours, *La Maniere de bien penser dans les ouvrages de l'esprit* (Paris: Veuve de S. Mabre-Cramoisy, 1687), pp. 300, 302.

9. J. Carel de Sainte-Garde, *Réflexions académiques sur les orateurs et sur les poètes* (Paris: C. Remy, 1676), p. 143.

10. Ibid., pp. 152, 156.

11. Ibid., pp. 159-60.

12. Ibid., pp. 152-53.

13. Quoted in Rousset, *L'Intérieur et l'extérieur*, p. 68.

14. Pierre Nicole, *Traité de la vraie et de la fausse beauté*, trans. into French by P. Richelet, in Bruzen de la Martinière, *Nouveau Recueil des épigrammatistes français* (Amsterdam: Wetstein, 1720), p. 187.

15. Antoine Arnauld and Pierre Nicole, *La Logique ou l'art de penser*, eds. P. Clair and F. Girbal (Paris: P.U.F., 1965), p. 96.

16. Ibid., pp. 99-100.

17. Ibid., p. 96.
18. F. Brunot and C. Bruneau, *Histoire de la langue française* (Paris: A. Colin, 1905-69), IIIa, 99.
19. Henri Estienne, *De la précellence du langage françois* (1579; rpt. Paris: Classiques Garnier, n.d.), pp. 246 ff.
20. Jacques Peletier, *L'Art poétique*, ed. André Boulanger (Paris: Les Belles Lettres, 1930), p. 125.
21. Quoted in Brunot, *Histoire*, I, 223.
22. Racan, p. 264.
23. Marie de Jars de Gournay, *Les Advis ou les présens de la demoiselle de Gournay* (Paris: Jean Du Bray, 1634), p. 467.
24. Ibid., p. 392.
25. Ibid., p. 449.
26. Jean Chapelain, *Lettres de Jean Chapelain*, ed. Ph. Tamizey de Larroque (Paris: Imprimerie Nationale, 1880-83), I, 17-20.
27. Gournay, *Advis*, p. 270.
28. Ibid., p. 482.
29. Antoine Arnauld, *Réflexions sur l'éloquence des prédicateurs* (Paris: F. and P. Delaulne, 1695), p. 133.
30. René Fromilhague, "La Création poétique chez Malherbe," *XVIIe Siècle*, No. 31 (April 1956), p. 264.
31. René Fromilhague, *Malherbe, technique et création poétique* (Paris: Armand Colin, 1954), and Claude K. Abraham, *Enfin Malherbe: The Influence of Malherbe on French Lyric Prosody, 1505-1674* (Lexington, Ky.: Univ. Press of Kentucky, 1971).
32. Brunot, *Histoire*, IIIa, 27.
33. Gournay, *Advis*, p. 421.
34. In Lucien Goldmann's reading of Racine in *Le Dieu caché* (Paris: Gallimard, "Bibliothèque des Idées," 1959).
35. Pellisson, *Histoire de l'académie française* (Paris: J.-B. Coignard fils, 1729), p. 86.
36. Francis Bar, *Le Genre burlesque en France au XVIIe siècle. Etude de style* (Paris: d'Artrey, 1960).
37. Saint-Amant, *Oeuvres complètes*, ed. Charles Livet (Paris: P. Jannet, 1855), II, 140.
38. I do not claim any historical link between Saint-Amant and the Jansenists, but it is at least curious that the Cospéan to whom *Le Contemplateur* is addressed was close to Saint-Cyran.
39. Gournay, *Advis*, p. 276.

BIBLIOGRAPHY

Editions

Saint-Amant. *Oeuvres*. Eds. Jean Lagny and Jacques Bailbé. 4 vols. Paris: Didier, STFM, 1967-71.
———. *Oeuvres complètes*. Ed. Charles Livet. 2 vols. Paris: P. Jannet, 1855.

Critical Studies on Saint-Amant

Bailbé, Jacques. "La Couleur baroque de la langue et du style dans les première œuvres de Saint-Amant." *Français Moderne*, 29 (1961), 43-61.
Borton, S.L. *Six Modes of Sensibility in Saint-Amant*. The Hague: Mouton, 1966.
Corum, Robert T., Jr. *Other Worlds and Other Seas: Art and Vision in Saint-Amant's Nature Poetry*. French Forum Monographs, 13. Lexington, Ky.: French Forum, Publishers, 1979.
Cosper, D. Dale. "Literary Pictorialism in the Short Idylls of Saint-Amant." *Papers on Seventeenth-Century French Literature*, 1 (1973), 1-3.
———. "Saint-Amant: Pictorialism and the Devotional Style." *Romance Notes*, 17 (Spring 1977), 286-97.
———. "The Literary Pictorialism of Saint-Amant." Diss. Univ. of Washington 1973.
Durand-Lapie, Paul. *Un Académicien du XVIIe siècle. Saint-Amant, son temps, sa vie, ses poésies, 1594-1661*. Paris: Delagrave, 1897.
Duval, Edwin M. *Poesis and Poetic Tradition in Early Works of Saint-Amant. Four Essays in Contextual Reading*. York, S.C.: French Literature Publications Company, 1980.
Gourier, Françoise. *Etude des œuvres poétiques de Saint-Amant*. Geneva: Droz, 1961.

128 THE LISTENING VOICE

Hafer, Nancy B.W. "The Art of Metaphor in La Ceppède's *Théorèmes* of 1613." Diss. Univ. of Virginia 1976.

Hallyn, Fernand. "Nature et rhétorique dans 'l'Hiver des Alpes' de Saint-Amant." *Les Lettres Romanes*, 25 (1971), 55-68.

Lagny, Jean. "Autour de la *Solitude* de Saint-Amant." *Bulletin du Bibliophile et du Bibliothécaire*, 1955, pp. 235-45; 1956, pp. 110-26.

———. *Bibliographie des éditions anciennes des œuvres de Saint-Amant.* Paris: Giraud-Badin, 1960.

———. *Le Poète Saint-Amant (1594-1661): essai sur sa vie et ses œuvres.* Paris: Nizet, 1964.

Lawrence, Francis L. "Time and the Individual Consciousness in Saint-Amant's *La Solitude* and *Le Contemplateur.*" *French Review*, 46, Special Issue No. 5 (Spring 1973), 32-40.

———. "Saint-Amant's 'L'Hyver des Alpes': A Structural Analysis." *Romanic Review*, 68 (1977), 247-53.

Lyons, John D. "*L'Andromède*: The Myth of the Poet and the Hero." *L'Esprit Créateur*, 16 (Summer 1976), 116-24.

———. "Saint-Amant's *La Solitude*: The Rhetoric of Fragmentation." *Orbis Litterarum*, 30 (1978), 4-17.

Le Hir, Yves. "Notes sur la langue et le style du *Moïse Sauvé* de Saint-Amant (1653)." *Français Moderne*, 19 (1951), 95-108.

Mazzara, Richard A. "A Case of Creative Imagination in Saint-Amant." *French Review*, 31 (1957), 27-34.

———. "Saint-Amant and the Italian Bernesque Poets." *French Review*, 32 (1959), 231-41.

———. "Saint-Amant's *L'Andromède* and Lope de Vega's *La Andromeda.*" *KFLQ*, 8 (1961), 7-14.

———. "The 'Anti-Hero' in Saint-Amant." *KFLQ*, 9 (1962), 123-29.

———. "Saint-Amant, Avant-garde Précieux Poet: 'La Jouyssance.'" *Ball State Teacher's College Forum*, 4 (1963), 58-63.

———. "Théophile de Viau, Saint-Amant, and the Spanish Soledad." *Kentucky Romance Quarterly*, 14 (1967), 393-404.

Rathé, Alice. "Saint-Amant, poète du 'caprice.'" *XVIIe Siècle*, No. 121 (1978), 229-44.

Ridgely, Beverly S. "Saint-Amant and 'The New Astronomy.'" *Modern Language Review*, 53 (1958), 26-37.

Roberts, W. "Classical Sources of Saint-Amant's *L'Arion.*" *French Studies*, 17 (1963), 341-50.

———. "Berni's 'Male Allogio' Motif in Saint-Amant." *Studi Francesi*, 27 (1965), 465-71.

Rolfe, C.D. *Saint-Amant and the Theory of Ut Pictura poesis.* London: M.H.R.A., 1972.

Romains, Jules. Preface to Saint-Amant, *Poésies baroques*. Coll. "Prestige de l'Académie française." Paris: Vialetay, 1969.
Root, Tamara G. "*La Solitude*: Saint-Amant's Expression of Unrest." *French Review*, 50 (1976), 12-20.
Rubin, David L. "Consciousness and the External World in A Caprice by Saint-Amant." *Yale French Studies*, 41 (1973), 170-77.
Sayce, R.A. "Saint-Amant and Poussin: ut pictura poesis." *French Studies*, 1 (1947), 241-51.
———. "Saint-Amant's *Moÿse sauvé*." In *The French Biblical Epic in the Seventeenth Century*. Oxford: The Clarendon Press, 1955.
Seznec, Alain. "Saint-Amant: le poète sauvé des eaux." In *Studies in Seventeenth-Century French Literature Presented to Morris Bishop*. Ed. J.-J. Demorest. Ithaca: Cornell Univ. Press, 1962 (rpt. Anchor Books, 1962), pp. 35-63.
Wencelius, M.S. "Contribution à l'étude du baroque: Saint-Amant." *XVIIe Siècle*, Nos. 5-6 (1959), 148-63.
Wentzlaff-Eggebert, Christian. *Forminteresse, Traditionsverbundenheit und Aktualisierungsberdürfnis als Merkmale des Dichtens von Saint-Amant*. Munich: Max Huebner, 1970.
———. "Le Fumeur." In *Die Französische Lyrik von Villon bis zur Gegenward*. Ed. H. Hinterhäuser. Düsseldorf: Bagel, 1975, I, pp. 171-80, 366-69.

General Criticism

Anon., ed. *Delle Rime Piacevoli del Borgogna, Ruscelli, Sansovino, Doni, Iasca, etc.*, Libro Terzo. Vicenza: Francesco Grossi, 1610.
Abraham, Claude K. *Enfin Malherbe: The Influence of Malherbe on French Lyric Prosody, 1605-1674*. Lexington: Univ. Press of Kentucky, 1971.
Argan, G. Carlo. *The Europe of the Capitals: 1600-1700*. Geneva: Skira, 1964.
Aristotle. *The Rhetoric of Aristotle*. Trans. Lane Cooper. New York: D. Appleton, 1932.
Arnauld, Antoine. *De la lecture de l'Ecriture sainte*. Antwerp: S. Matthieu, 1680.
———. *Réflexions sur l'éloquence des prédicateurs*. Paris: F. and P. Delaulne, 1695.
———, and Pierre Nicole. *La Logique ou l'Art de penser*. Eds. P. Clair and F. Girbal. Paris: P.U.F., 1965.
———, and Claude Lancelot. *Grammaire générale et raisonnée*. 1660; rpt. Paris: Paulet, 1969.

Bal, Mieke. "Narration et focalisation." *Poétique,* 29 (February 1977), 107-27.

Balzac, Jean Louis Guez de. *Oeuvres.* Ed. Valentin Conrart. Paris: L. Billaine, 1665.

Bar, Francis. *Le Genre burlesque en France au XVIIe siècle. Etude de style.* Paris: d'Artrey, 1960.

Barthes, Roland. *S/Z.* Paris: Seuil, 1970.

———. "Loyola." In *Sade, Fourier, Loyola.* Paris: Seuil, 1971, pp. 45-80.

——— et al. *Exégèse et herméneutique.* Paris: Seuil, 1971.

Baruzi, Jean. *Saint Jean de la Croix et le problème de l'expérience mystique.* Paris: Alcan, 1924.

Beverly, John R. "Soledad Primera, lines 1-61." *MLN,* 88 (March 1973), 233-48.

Block, Haskell M. "The Alleged Parallel of Metaphysical and Symbolist Poetry." *Comparative Literature Studies,* 4 (1967), 145-60.

Booth, Wayne C. *The Rhetoric of Fiction.* Chicago: Univ. of Chicago Press, 1961.

———. *Critical Understanding. The Powers and Limits of Pluralism.* Chicago: Univ. of Chicago Press, 1979.

Borgerhoff, E.B.O. *The Freedom of French Classicism.* Princeton: Princeton Univ. Press, 1950.

Bouhours, le Père Dominique. *Entretiens d'Ariste et d'Eugène.* Paris: S. Mabre-Cramoisy, 1671.

———. *Doutes sur la langue françoise proposez à Messieurs de l'Académie françoise par un gentilhomme de province.* Paris: S. Mabre-Cramoisy, 1674.

———. *La Manière de bien penser dans les ouvrages de l'esprit.* Paris: Veuve de S. Mabre-Cramoisy, 1687.

Bray, René. *La Formation de la doctrine classique en France.* 1927; rpt. Paris: Nizet, 1951.

Brébeuf, Georges de. *Oeuvres.* Paris: Jean Ribou, 1664.

Bremond, Henri. *Histoire littéraire du sentiment religieux en France.* Paris: Bloud & Gay, 1916-33.

Brisca, Lidia Menapace. "L'Arguta e ingegnosa elocuzione: appunti per una lettura del Cannocchiale Aristotelico di E. Tesauro." *AEvum,* 28 (1954), 45-60.

Brunot, Ferdinand. *La Doctrine de Malherbe d'après son commentaire sur Desportes.* 1891; rpt. Paris: A. Colin, 1969.

———. *Histoire de la langue française des origines à 1900.* Paris: A. Colin, 1905-69.

Buffum, Imbrie. *Studies in the Baroque from Montaigne to Rotrou.* New Haven: Yale Univ. Press, 1957.

BIBLIOGRAPHY   131

Carel de Sainte-Garde, J. *Réflexions académiques sur les orateurs et sur les poètes*. Paris: C. Remy, 1676.

———. *Histoire des hérésies et des hérétiques*. Paris: C. Barbin, 1697.

Cavalluzzi, Raffaele. "Il Gioco e la vertigine (di alcune condizioni strutturali della lirica mariniana)." *Trimestre*, 5 (1971), 329-56.

Cave, Terence C. *Devotional Poetry in France, 1570-1613*. Cambridge: Cambridge Univ. Press, 1969.

———. *The Cornucopian Text: Problems of Writing in the French Renaissance*. Oxford: The Clarendon Press, 1979.

Chapelain, Jean. "Lettre ou Discours de M. Chapelain à M. Favereau . . . portant son opinion sur le poëme d'Adonis." In G.B. Marino, *L'Adone poema*. Paris: n.p., 1623.

———. *De la lecture des vieux romans*. Ed. Alphonse Feillet. Paris: A. Abury, 1870.

———. *Lettres de Jean Chapelain*. Ed. Ph. Tamizey de Larroque. Paris: Imprimerie Nationale, 1880-1883.

———. *Lettres inédites de Jean Chapelain à P.-D. Huet*. Ed. G. Pélissier. Nogent-le-Rotrou: Daupeley-Gouverneur, 1894.

Charpentier, F. *Carpenteriana*. Amsterdam, 1741.

Charpentrat, P. *Le Mirage baroque*. Coll. "Critique." Paris: Minuit: 1967.

Chatman, Seymour, ed. *Literary Style: A Symposium*. London: Oxford Univ. Press, 1971.

Chevreau, Urbain. "Remarques." In *Les Oeuvres de François de Malherbe*. Paris: Barbou, 1722.

Coëffeteau, Nicolas. *Tableau des passions humaines*. Paris: S. Cramoisy, 1620.

Cohen, J.M. *The Baroque Lyric*. London: Hutchinson, 1963.

Colie, Rosalie. "*My Echoing Song*": *Andrew Marvell's Poetry of Criticism*. Princeton: Princeton Univ. Press, 1970.

Colletet, Guillaume. *Discours du poëme bucolique*. Paris: Chamhoudry, 1657.

———. *Discours contre la traduction*. Paris: Sommaville, 1658.

———. *Discours de l'éloquence et de l'imitation des anciens*. Paris: Sommaville, 1658.

———. *Traitté de la poésie morale et sententieuse*. Paris: Sommaville, 1658.

———. *Traitté de l'épigramme*. Paris: Sommaville, 1658.

———. *Traitté du sonnet*. Paris: Sommaville, 1658.

Conte, Gian Biagio. *Memoria dei poeti e sistema letterario*. Turin: Einaudi, 1974.

Conti, Natale. *Mythologie, c'est-à-dire explication des fables*. French trans. by J. de Montlyard. Lyons: Frelon, 1604.

Crawford, J.P. Wickersham. "The Setting of Góngora's *Las Soledades.*" *Hispanic Review*, 3 (1939), 347-49.

Dalla Valle, Daniela. *La Frattura: Studi sul barocco letterario francese.* Ravenna: A. Longo, 1970.

Davity, Pierre. *Les Travaux sans travail.* Lyons: T. Ancelin, 1603.

De Girancourt, A. *Nouvelle Etude sur la verrerie de Rouen.* Rouen: Cagniard, 1886.

Deimier, Pierre de. *L'Académie de l'art poétique.* Paris: J. de Bordeaulx, 1610.

Delley, Gilbert. *L'Assomption de la nature dans la lyrique française de l'âge baroque.* Berne: H. Lang, 1969.

Delorme, J. *Le Langage de la foi dans l'Ecriture et dans le monde actuel.* Paris: Cerf, 1972.

De Mourgues, Odette. *Metaphysical, Baroque and Précieux Poetry.* Oxford: Clarendon Press, 1953.

———. *O Muse, fuyante proie . . . Essai sur la poésie de La Fontaine.* Paris: Corti, 1962.

Desmarets de Saint-Sorlin, J. *La Défense du poème héroique, Dialogues.* Paris: Claude Audinet, 1674.

———. *La Défense de la poésie et de la langue françoise, addressée à Monsieur Perrault.* Paris: N. Le Gras, 1675.

D'Ors, Eugenio. *Du baroque.* French trans. (1935). Rpt. Paris: Gallimard, 1968.

Dubois, J. et al. *Rhétorique générale.* Paris: Larousse, 1970.

DuPerron, J.D. Cardinal. *Perroniana.* Cologne, 1694.

Durand, Laura G. "Sponde and Donne: Lens and Prism." *Comparative Literature*, 21 (1969), 319-36.

Duvignaud, Jean. "Le Mythe baroque." *Nouvelle Revue Française*, 26 (1965), 708-15.

Eco, Umberto. *A Theory of Semiotics.* Bloomington: Indiana Univ. Press, 1976.

Faguet, Emile. *Histoire de la poésie française.* Paris: Boivin, 1927-36.

Forster, Leonard. *The Icy Fire. Five Studies in European Petrarchism.* Cambridge: Cambridge Univ. Press, 1969.

Fromilhague, René. *Malherbe, technique et création poétique.* Paris: A. Colin, 1954.

Foucault, M. *Les Mots et les choses.* Paris: Gallimard, 1966.

———. *L'Ordre du discours.* Paris: Gallimard, 1970.

Fournel, Victor. *La Littérature indépendante et les écrivains oubliés.* Paris: Didier, 1862.

Gautier, Théophile. *Les Grotesques* (1844). Paris: Michel Lévy, 1871.

Genette, Gérard. *Figures*. 3 vols. Paris: Seuil, 1966-72.

Godeau, Antoine. "Discours sur les œuvres de Malherbe." In *Les Oeuvres de Monsieur François de Malherbe*. Paris: C. Chappellain, 1630.

Gournay, Marie de Jars de. *Les Advis ou les Présens de la demoiselle de Gournay*. Paris: Jean Du Bray, 1634.

Greene, Thomas. *The Descent from Heaven. A Study in Continuity*. New Haven: Yale Univ. Press, 1963.

Greimas, A.J. *Sémantique structurale*. Paris: Larousse, 1969.

Guillén, Claudio. *Literature as System: Essays Toward the Theory of Literary History*. Princeton: Princeton Univ. Press, 1971.

Jakobson, Roman. *Essais de linguistique générale*. Paris: Minuit, 1963.

———. *Questions de poétique*. Paris: Seuil, 1973.

Jeanneret, Michel. *Poésie et tradition biblique au XVIe siècle*. Paris: J. Corti, 1969.

Jolles, A. *Formes simples* (1930). French trans. by A.M. Buguet. Paris: Seuil, 1972.

Hatzfeld, Helmut. "Mannerism is not Baroque." *L'Esprit Créateur*, 6 (Winter 1966), 225-33.

Hubert, Judd D. "Myth and Status: Malherbe's Swan Song." *Yale French Studies*, 49 (1973), 132-42.

Kermode, Frank. "The Argument of Marvell's 'Garden.'" *Essays in Criticism*, 2 (July 1952), 225-41.

Kibédi Varga, A. "La Poésie religieuse au XVIIe siècle: suggestions et cadres d'études." *Neophilologus*, 46 (November 1962), 263-78.

———. *Rhétorique et littérature: études de structures classiques*. Paris: Didier, 1970.

Kristeva, Julia. "L'Engendrement de la formule." In *Semiotiho*. Paris: Seuil, 1969, pp. 278-371.

La Mothe le Vayer, François de. *Observations diverses sur la composition et sur la lecture des livres*. Paris: L. Billaine, 1668.

Lamy, Bernard. *Nouvelles Réflexions sur l'art poétique*. Paris, 1678.

Lanson, Gustave. *Histoire illustrée de la littérature française*. Paris: Hachette, 1923.

La Pinelière. *Le Parnasse ou la critique des poètes*. Paris: T. Quinet, 1635.

Lapp, John C. "Mythological Imagery as Counterpoint." In *French Renaissance Studies in Honor of Isidore Silver*. Ed. Frieda S. Brown. *Kentucky Romance Quarterly*, 20 (1974), Supplement No. 2, 265-82.

Laudin d'Aigaliers, Pierre de. *L'Art poétique françois*. Paris: Anthoine du Brueil, 1598.

Lebègue, Raymond. "Quelques Thèmes de la poésie lyrique au temps de Louis XIII." *XVIIe Siècle*, No. 66-67 (1965), 7-21.

Leblanc, P. *Les Paraphrases françaises des Psaumes (1610-1660)*. Paris: P.U.F., 1960.

Le Maistre, Martial. *Le Procès du melon*. Paris, 1607.

Lotman, Iouri. *La Structure du texte artistique*. French trans. by Henri Meschonnic et al. "Bibliothèque des Sciences Humaines." Paris: Gallimard, 1973.

Lyons, Bridget Gellert. *Voices of Melancholy*. New York: Barnes and Noble, 1971.

Mâle, Emile. *L'Art religieux après le concile de Trente*. Paris: A. Colin, 1932:

Marin, Louis. *Etudes sémiologiques. Ecritures, peintures*. Paris: Klincksieck, 1971.

――――. *Sémiotique de la passion*. Paris: Desclée de Brouwer, 1971.

――――. "A propos d'un carton de Le Brun: le tableau d'histoire ou la dégénération de l'énonciation." *Revue des Sciences Humaines*, 40, No. 157 (January-March 1975), 41-64.

――――. "Ecriture/peinture: l'ex-voto de Champaigne." In *Vers une esthétique sans entrave. Mélanges Mikel Dufrenne*. Paris: Union Générale d'Edition, 1975, pp. 409-29.

――――, and Claude Chabrol, eds. *Le Récit évangélique*. Paris: Desclée de Brouwer, 1971.

――――. "Sémiotique narrative: récits bibliques." *Langages*, 20 (June 1971).

Marino, Giovan Battista. *Marino e i marinisti*. Ed. G.G. Ferrero. Milan: Riccardo Ricciardi, 1954.

Marolles, Michel de. *Mémoires*. Paris: Sommaville, 1656-57.

――――. *Traité du poème épique pour l'intelligence de l'Enéide*. Paris: de Luyne, 1662.

Martz, Louis L. *The Poetry of Meditation*. New Haven: Yale Univ. Press, 1954. Rev. ed., 1962.

McCanles, Michael. *Dialectical Criticism and Renaissance Literature*. Berkeley and Los Angeles: Univ. of California Press, 1975.

Ménage, Gilles. *Le Parnasse alarmé*. Paris, 1649.

――――. *Menagiana*. Amsterdam: A. Braakman, 1693.

――――. "Observations." In *Les Oeuvres de François de Malherbe*. Paris: Barbou, 1722.

Méré, Le chevalier de [Antoine Gombauld]. *Oeuvres complètes*. Ed. Charles-H. Boudhors. "Les Textes Français." Paris: F. Roches, 1930.

Michaelson, Erik. "L'Eau, centre de métaphores et de métamorphoses dans la littérature française de la première moitié du XVIIe siècle. Le miroir de l'eau et le déluge." *Orbis Litterarum*, 14 (1959), 121-73.

Miner, Earl. *The Metaphysical Mode from Donne to Cowley*. Princeton: Princeton Univ. Press, 1969.

Mirollo, James V. *The Poet of the Marvelous: Giambattista Marino.* New York: Columbia Univ. Press, 1963.

Molho, Maurice. *Sémantique et poétique: à propos des solitudes de Góngora.* Bordeaux: Ducros, 1969.

Mollet, Claude. *Le Théâtre des plans et jardinages.* Paris: Ch. de Sercy, 1652.

Mongrédien, G. *Etudes sur la vie et l'œuvre de N. Vauquelin, seigneur des Yveteaux.* Paris: Picard, 1921.

Nelson, Lowry, Jr. *Baroque Lyric Poetry.* New Haven: Yale Univ. Press, 1961.

Nichols, Stephen G., Jr., and F.W. Robinson, eds. *The Meaning of Mannerism.* Hanover, N.H.: Univ. Press of New England, 1972.

Nicole, Pierre. "Traité de la vraie et de la fausse beauté." French trans. by P. Richelet. In Bruzen de la Martinière, *Nouveau Recueil des épigrammatistes français.* Amsterdam: Wetstein, 1720.

Ong, Walter J. "The Writer's Audience is Always a Fiction." *PMLA,* 90 (January 1975), 9-21.

Panofsky, Erwin. *Galileo as a Critic of the Arts.* The Hague: M. Nijhoff, 1954.

———. *A Mythological Painting by Poussin.* Stockholm: National-musei Skriftserie, No. 5, 1960.

Pedersen, John. *Images et figures dans la poésie française de l'âge baroque.* Copenhagen: Akademia Verlag, 1974. *Revue Romane,* Spec. Issue, No. 5.

Peiresc, C.-N. Fabri de. *Lettres à sa famille.* Ed. Ph. Tamizey de Larroque. Paris: Imprimerie Nationale, 1893-96.

———. *Lettres aux Frères Dupuy.* Ed. Ph. Tamizey de Larroque. Paris: Imprimerie Nationale, 1888-92.

Peletier, Jacques. *L'Art poétique.* Ed. André Boulanger. Paris: Les Belles Lettres, 1930.

Pellison-Fontanier, P. *Histoire de l'Académie française.* Paris: J.-B. Coignard fils, 1729.

Perrault, Charles. *Les Murs de Troye, ou l'origine du burlesque.* Paris: Chamhoudry, 1653.

———. *Parallèle des Anciens et des Modernes.* Paris: J.-B. Coignard, 1688-92.

Peters, S.N. "Metaphor and 'Maraviglia': Tradition and Innovation in the 'Adone' of G.B. Marino." *Lingua e Stile,* 7 (1972), 321-41.

Pons, Jacques. *Traité des melons.* Rev. ed. Lyons: Antoine Cellier fils, 1680.

Poulet, Georges. *Les Métamorphoses du cercle.* Paris: Plon, 1961.

Praz, Mario. *Studies in Seventeenth Century Imagery.* Rev. ed. Rome: Edizioni di Storia e Letteratura, 1974-75.

Racan, H. de B. *Anecdotes inédites sur Malherbe.* Ed. Louis Arnould. Paris: Picard, 1893.

Rapin, René. *Réflexions sur la poétique d'Aristote et sur les ouvrages des poètes anciens et modernes.* Paris: Muguet, 1674.

——— [attributed]. *L'Oraison sans illusions: contre les erreurs de la fausse contemplation.* Paris: E. Michallet, 1687.

Raymond, Marcel. *Baroque et Renaissance poétique.* Paris: Corti, 1955.

———, and A.J. Steele. *La Poésie française et le maniérisme.* Geneva: Droz, 1971.

Réau, Louis. *Iconographie de la Bible. Nouveau Testament.* Paris: P.U.F., 1957.

Relyea, Suzanne. *Signs, Systems, and Meanings.* Middletown: Wesleyan Univ. Press, 1976.

Riffaterre, Michael. *Essais de stylistique structurale.* Trans. Daniel Delas. Paris: Flammarion, 1971.

———. "Interpretation and Descriptive Poetry: A Reading of Wordsworth's 'Yew-Trees.'" *New Literary History,* 4, No. 2 (Winter 1973), 229-56.

———. *Semiotics of Poetry.* Bloomington: Indiana Univ. Press, 1978.

Rigolot, François. "Rhétorique du nom poétique." *Poétique,* 28 (1976), 466-83.

Rousset, Jean. *La Littérature de l'âge baroque en France.* Paris: Corti, 1954.

———. *L'Intérieur et l'extérieur.* Paris: Corti, 1968.

Rubin, David Lee. *A Higher, Hidden Order: Design and Meaning in the Odes of Malherbe.* Chapel Hill: Univ. of North Carolina Studies in Romance Languages and Literatures, 1972.

Sainte-Beuve, C.A. *Les Grands Ecrivains français, XVIIe siècle. Les poètes.* Paris: Garnier, 1927.

Salques, Marie-France. "Spectacle et représentation dans l'Adone de Giovan Battista Marino." *Revue des Sciences Humaines,* 37, No. 145 (January-March 1972), 69-90.

Schaff, Adam. *Introduction à la sémantique.* Paris: Anthropos, 1974.

Schmidt, A.M. "Constants baroques dans la littérature française." *Trivium,* 7 (1949), 309-24.

———. *L'Amour noir: poèmes baroques.* Monaco: Editions du Rocher, 1959.

Schwenger, Peter. "Crashaw's Perspectivist Metaphor." *Comparative Literature,* 28 (Winter 1976), 65-74.

Searle, J.R. *Speech-Acts.* Cambridge: Cambridge Univ. Press, 1969.

Sebeok, Thomas, ed. *Style in Language.* Cambridge, Mass.: The M.I.T. Press, 1960.

Simone, Franco. *Umanesimo, Rinascimento, Barocco in Francia.* Milan: Mursia, 1968.

Simpson, J.C. *Le Tasse et la littérature et l'art baroques en France.* Paris: Nizet, 1962.

Smith, Barbara H. *Poetic Closure: A Study of How Poems End.* 1968; rpt. Chicago: Univ. of Chicago Press, 1970.

Sperber, Dan. *Le Symbolisme en général.* Paris: Hermann, 1974.

Steele, A. J. " 'A la claire fontaine'—Aspects de la poésie de l'eau au XVIIe siècle." *CAIEF,* 6 (July 1954), 57-74.

Strawson, P.F. "On Referring." *Mind,* 59 (1950), 320-44.

Sypher, Wylie. *Four Stages of Renaissance Style.* New York: Doubleday, Anchor Books, 1955.

Tertulian, Nicolas. "Sur l'autonomie et l'hétéronomie de l'art." *Revue d'Esthétique,* No. 2-3 (1976), 110-39.

Tesauro, Emanuele. *Il Cannocchiale Aristotelico.* Bad Homburg: Verlag Gehlen, 1968 (facsimile of 1670 Torino edition).

Thuillier, Jacques et al. *La Peinture française.* Geneva: Skira, 1963-74.

Tiefenbrun, Susan W. "Mathurin Régnier's *Macette*: A Semiotic Study in Satire." *Semiotica,* 13, No. 2 (1975), 131-53.

Todorov, Tzevetan. "Les Registres de la parole." *Journal de Psychologie,* 64, No. 3 (1967), 265-78.

———. "Poétique." In O. Ducrot et al., *Qu'est-ce que le structuralisme?* Paris: Seuil, 1968.

Valesio, Paolo. *Novantiqua. Rhetorics as a Contemporary Theory.* Bloomington: Indiana Univ. Press, 1980.

Vaugelas, Claude Favre, Sieur de. *Remarques sur la langue française.* Geneva: Droz, 1934 (facsimile of the 1647 edition).

Vinet, Elle, and Antoine Mizauld. *La Maison champestre.* Paris. Robert Foüet, 1607.

Warman, Stephen. "The Subject-Matter and Treatment of Marino's Images." *Studi Seicenteschi,* 10 (1969), 57-131.

———. "Marinist Imagery in French Poetry, 1607-1650." *Studi Seicenteschi,* 12 (1971), 117-76.

Warnke, F.J. *European Metaphysical Poetry.* New Haven: Yale Univ. Press, 1961.

———. *Versions of Baroque.* New Haven: Yale Univ. Press, 1972.

Weinrich, Harald. *Le Temps.* French trans. by M. Lacoste. Paris: Seuil, 1973.

Wellek, René. "The Concept of Baroque in Literary Scholarship." *Journal of Aesthetics and Art Criticism,* 5 (1946), 77-109.

Winegarten, Renee. *French Lyric Poetry in the Age of Malherbe*. Manchester: Manchester Univ. Press, 1954.

Wölfflin, Heinrich. *Renaissance and Baroque* (1888). Trans. Kathrin Smith. 1966; rpt. Ithaca: Cornell Univ. Press, 1967.

FRENCH FORUM MONOGRAPHS

1. Karolyn Waterson. *Molière et l'autorité: Structures sociales, structures comiques.* 1976.
2. Donna Kuizenga. *Narrative Strategies in* La Princesse de Clèves. 1976.
3. Ian J. Winter. *Montaigne's Self-Portrait and Its Influence in France, 1580-1630.* 1976.
4. Judith G. Miller. *Theater and Revolution in France since 1968.* 1977.
5. Raymond C. La Charité, ed. *O un amy! Essays on Montaigne in Honor of Donald M. Frame.* 1977.
6. Rupert T. Pickens. *The Welsh Knight: Paradoxicality in Chrétien's* Conte del Graal. 1977.
7. Carol Clark. *The Web of Metaphor: Studies in the Imagery of Montaigne's* Essais. 1978.
8. Donald Maddox. *Structure and Sacring: The Systematic Kingdom in Chrétien's* Erec et Enide. 1978.
9. Betty J. Davis. *The Storytellers in Marguerite de Navarre's* Heptaméron. 1978.
10. Laurence M. Porter. *The Renaissance of the Lyric in French Romanticism: Elegy, "Poëme" and Ode.* 1978.
11. Bruce R. Leslie. *Ronsard's Successful Epic Venture: The Epyllion.* 1979.
12. Michelle A. Freeman. *The Poetics of* Translatio Studii *and* Conjointure: Chrétien de Troyes's Cligés. 1979.
13. Robert T. Corum, Jr. *Other Worlds and Other Seas: Art and Vision in Saint-Amant's Nature Poetry.* 1979.
14. Marcel Muller. *Préfiguration et structure romanesque dans* A la recherche du temps perdu *(avec un inédit de Marcel Proust).* 1979.
15. Ross Chambers. *Meaning and Meaningfulness: Studies in the Analysis and Interpretation of Texts.* 1979.
16. Lois Oppenheim. *Intentionality and Intersubjectivity: A Phenomenological Study of Butor's* La Modification. 1980.
17. Matilda T. Bruckner. *Narrative Invention in Twelfth-Century French Romance: The Convention of Hospitality (1160-1200).* 1980.
18. Gérard Defaux. *Molière, ou les métamorphoses du comique. De la comédie morale au triomphe de la folie.* 1980.
19. Raymond C. La Charité. *Recreation, Reflection and Re-Creation: Perspectives on Rabelais's* Pantagruel. 1980.
20. Jules Brody. *Du style à la pensée: Trois études sur les* Caractères de La Bruyère. 1980.
21. Lawrence D. Kritzman. *Destruction/Découverte: Le Fonctionnement de la rhétorique dans les* Essais de Montaigne. 1980.
22. Minnette Grunmann-Gaudet and Robin F. Jones, eds. *The Nature of Medieval Narrative.* 1980.
23. J.A. Hiddleston. *Essai sur Laforgue et les* Derniers Vers suivi de Laforgue et Baudelaire. 1980.
24. Michael S. Koppisch. *The Dissolution of Character: Changing Perspectives in La Bruyère's* Caractères. 1981.
25. Hope H. Glidden. *The Storyteller as Humanist: The* Serées of Guillaume Bouchet. 1981.
26. Mary B. McKinley. *Words in a Corner: Studies in Montaigne's Latin Quotations.* 1981.

27. Donald M. Frame and Mary B. McKinley, eds. *Columbia Montaigne Conference Papers*. 1981.
28. Jean-Pierre Dens. *L'Honnête Homme et la critique du goût: Esthétique et société au XVIIe siècle*. 1981.
29. Vivian Kogan. *The Flowers of Fiction: Time and Space in Raymond Queneau's Les Fleurs bleues*. 1982.
30. Michael Issacharoff et Jean-Claude Vilquin, éds. *Sartre et la mise en signe*. 1982.
31. James W. Mileham. *The Conspiracy Novel: Structure and Metaphor in Balzac's Comédie humaine*. 1982.
32. Andrew G. Suozzo, Jr. *The Comic Novels of Charles Sorel: A Study of Structure, Characterization and Disguise*. 1982.
33. Margaret Whitford. *Merleau-Ponty's Critique of Sartre's Philosophy*. 1982.
34. Gérard Defaux. *Le Curieux, le glorieux et la sagesse du monde dans la première moitié du XVIe siècle: L'exemple de Panurge (Ulysse, Démosthène, Empédocle)*. 1982.
35. Doranne Fenoaltea. *"Si haulte Architecture." The Design of Scève's Délie*. 1982.
36. Peter Bayley and Dorothy Gabe Coleman, eds. *The Equilibrium of Wit: Essays for Odette de Mourgues*. 1982.
37. Carol J. Murphy. *Alienation and Absence in the Novels of Marguerite Duras*. 1982.
38. Mary Ellen Birkett. *Lamartine and the Poetics of Landscape*. 1982.
39. Jules Brody. *Lectures de Montaigne*. 1982.
40. John D. Lyons. *The Listening Voice: An Essay on the Rhetoric of Saint-Amant*. 1982.

French Forum, Publishers, Inc.
P.O. Box 5108, Lexington, Kentucky 40505

Publishers of *French Forum*, a journal of literary criticism